EVERYDAY GUIDES
MADE EASY

FINALE
MUSIC APP
BASICS

This is a **FLAME TREE** book
First published 2015

Publisher and Creative Director: Nick Wells
Project Editor: Polly Prior
Art Director and Layout Design: Mike Spender
Digital Design and Production: Chris Herbert
Screenshots: Ben Byram-Wigfield
Copy Editor: Anna Groves
Technical Editor: Ronan Macdonald
Proofreader: Dawn Laker
Indexer: Helen Snaith

Special thanks to: Josie Mitchell

This edition first published 2015 by
FLAME TREE PUBLISHING
Crabtree Hall, Crabtree Lane
Fulham, London SW6 6TY
United Kingdom

www.flametreepublishing.com

© 2015 Flame Tree Publishing

15 17 19 18 16
1 3 5 7 9 10 8 6 4 2

ISBN 978-1-78361-395-3

Printed in China

Image Credits: Courtesy Ben Byram-Wigfield and Flame Tree Publishing, 26.
All other *non-screenshot* pictures are courtesy of **iStock** and © the following
contributors: enjoynz 1,3; ValuaVitaly 5; dp_photo 7; mstay 8; gpointstudio 18;
PeopleImages 19; annebaek 20; annebaek 22; tomhoryn 28; RapidEye 30;
VOLYK IEVGENII 38; RKaulitzki 50; pagadesign 56; MarsBars 58; stocknroll 62;
tonivaver 63; hidesy 66; kutberk 67; onurdongel 69; ValuaVitaly 70; sandsun 80;
traffic_analyzer 83; SelectStock 84; DragonImages 93; Alhovik 95; alengo 100;
loonger 102; PhotoEuphoria 110; andresr 111; -lvinst- 112; kupicoo 121;
ricardoinfante 122; alvarez 126

EVERYDAY GUIDES
MADE EASY

FINALE
MUSIC APP
BASICS

BEN BYRAM-WIGFIELD

FLAME TREE
PUBLISHING

CONTENTS

How to get familiar with the application and start a new document.

An introduction to the different ways of entering notes, percussion symbols
and guitar tablature into your score.

A guide to adding notation symbols to your music: lyrics, expressions,
articulations, dynamics, slurs and other shapes.

How to move, copy, delete, correct and adjust parts of your score,
as well as lay out the music on to pages.

A guide to all the things you can do with your score when it's complete:
exporting to other formats and working with audio playback.

An introduction to the powerful capabilities of Finale: tools for fine
adjustments and plug-ins for special tasks.

SERIES FOREWORD

While the unstoppable rise of computer technology has left no area of the creative arts untouched, perhaps the most profoundly transformed of them all is music. From performance, composition and production to marketing, distribution and playback, the Apple Mac and Windows PC – and, more recently, their increasingly capable smartphone and tablet cousins – have given anyone, no matter what their budget, the ability to create professional-quality tracks in the comfort of their own home and put them online for the whole world to hear.

Compositional tools like Sibelius and Finale put more music notation power at your fingertips than you could ever hope to match with ink and paper. What's rather more difficult to come by, though, is the knowledge required to put them to effective use – which is where this book comes in.

A comprehensive guide to Finale, taking you through all the key concepts in a succinct, easy-to-understand way, *Finale Music App Basics* is sure to serve as a trusty companion on your music-making journey, whether you're a total beginner or a more advanced producer looking to brush up on the basics. Work through it methodically from start to finish, or keep it by your side for reference – just don't forget to give us a credit on your debut album!

Ronan Macdonald
Music technology writer and editor

INTRODUCTION

Finale is a professional app for producing music notation. It combines many features usually found in DTP software, graphics programs and audio workstations. It can notate a symphony or a guitar lead sheet, a simple piano sonata or some *avant-garde* spectacle.

Above: Finale's mobile app, SongBook, enables you to view your music on the go.

FIRST-TIME FINALE

In order to produce the different notation that musicians want to write, Finale has a large assortment of settings, preferences, tools and options. This gives Finale an incredible flexibility, but can leave the first-time user feeling daunted.

This book will help you to get started with Finale, and guide you through the process of creating a new score. It will show you how to enter notes and other symbols, and how to lay out your music on the page. Once your score is complete, it will outline how to use your score for playback and how to export it to other formats.

FINALE VERSIONS

Finale runs on both Windows and Mac. The app is almost identical on each platform, though some of the keyboard shortcuts are

Above: Finale will help turn the tune in your head into a professional-looking score.

different. Up until 2012, new versions of the app were released every year, each with new features. However, since then, the app is being released roughly every two years. The current version is Finale 2014.

Finale also has several 'sibling' products – versions of the same software that have fewer features at a reduced price. There is Finale NotePad, Finale SongWriter and Finale PrintMusic in addition to 'full' Finale. There is also an app for viewing Finale files on Apple's iPad, Finale SongBook.

Hot Tips

Look out for hot tips to get even more out of your Finale experience: from quick shortcuts to pro advice for more advanced users.

GETTING STARTED

Finale is available as a download, or on a DVD, and installs much like any other software, with a series of steps to click through. Once that's done, you're all set to start writing music!

SETTING UP A MIDI KEYBOARD

From version 2012 onwards, Finale automatically detects MIDI devices attached to your computer. The first time you launch Finale, a MIDI Setup dialog will appear, where you can check that your devices are listed.

Below: The MIDI Setup dialog will detect the MIDI devices that are linked to your computer.

FONTS

Finale installs several fonts into your system in order to display a wide range of music symbols in a number of different styles. You can use them in other apps too.

AUTHORIZATION

To prevent software piracy, your copy of Finale must be registered with MakeMusic (the company that makes Finale). Authorization can be done over an internet connection, using the 'Authorize Finale' command in the Help menu. Finale will run for 30 days without authorization before saving and printing are disabled. You can install two authorized copies on any computers that you own. If you want to use Finale on a new computer, you need to deauthorize the old hardware before authorizing the new one. You only need to do this step once.

```
┌─────────────────────────────────────────────────────────────┐
│                   Finale Authorization Wizard                │
├─────────────────────────────────────────────────────────────┤
│ Authorizing your copy of Finale is quick and easy! Authorize to receive: │
│                                                              │
│              • Free Technical Support                        │
│              • Free Maintenance releases                     │
│              • Discounts on future upgrades and new products │
│              • Important product information                 │
│                                                              │
│              An internet connection is recommended           │
│         Please disable any firewalls until authorization is complete. │
│                                                              │
│       First Name: [                    ]                     │
│        Last Name: [                    ]                     │
│    Serial Number: [          ]  [ What is my Serial Number? ]│
│                    XXXX-XXXXXXXX                             │
│                                                              │
│ [ Cancel ]                              [ < Back ] [ Next > ]│
└─────────────────────────────────────────────────────────────┘
```

Above: Follow the instructions in the Registration dialog box to authorize your copy of Finale.

TERMINOLOGY

A basic knowledge of music terms is assumed, but to get the most out of this book, there are a few things that you need to know.

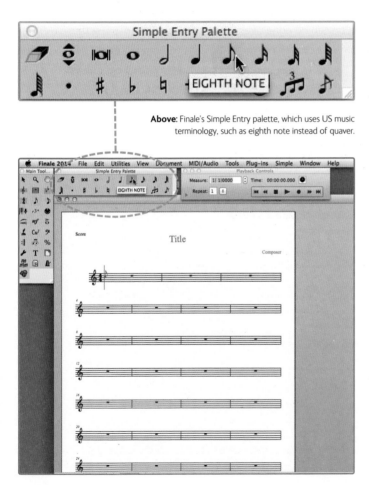

Above: Finale's Simple Entry palette, which uses US music terminology, such as eighth note instead of quaver.

US VERSUS UK

Being an American program, Finale uses American music terminology, which has a few differences from terms used in the UK. Finale uses the term 'measure' where we would normally say 'bar'. Note values use terms such as 'half note' instead of 'minim'; 'quarter note' instead of 'crotchet'; and 'eighth note' instead of 'quaver'. However, whenever you need to select a note value, there are always images of the note to guide you if you're uncertain.

STAFF

A staff is one line of music, usually for one instrument. Some instruments, like the piano, use two staves joined together, called 'the grand stave'.

SYSTEM

A system is one group of connected staves and measures on a page. A page will typically contain one or more systems.

Hot Tip

Note that the plural of staff is staves!

Above: This document window shows six measures, four staves and two systems.

METATOOL

Finale's own documentation refers to 'metatools' a lot, which sounds a bit arcane. This is simply another name for a keyboard shortcut that the user can configure. The app uses a lot of keyboard shortcuts, and by learning the ones for the functions that you use frequently, you can get quick results; we cover these in more detail on pages 122–123.

LAUNCH WINDOW

Every time you launch Finale, you will see the Launch Window. There are many ways of starting to work with a document in Finale, and you can control them all from here. Alternatively, you can close the Launch Window and access the same features from the File menu.

Above: Finale's Launch Window, which you will see each time you open the application.

Hot Tip

You can configure what Finale does at launch in Preferences > New.

SETUP WIZARD

The Setup Wizard is a series of four dialogs that help you build up a new document. It's the easiest way to create scores with several instrumental (or vocal) staves, and to get your document ready for entering notes. We'll discuss it in detail later on.

DEFAULT DOCUMENT

This is the document on which Finale bases all new documents. You can open a copy of it in the Launch Window, as a clean, basic document on which to start your work. You can also modify it to your own specifications and re-save it into the Defaults folder, so that all new documents will be based on your version.

TEMPLATES

Finale comes with a huge array of ready-made templates for a variety of ensembles and styles. There are templates for choirs, for marching bands, for full orchestras or individual instruments. You can create your own templates and add them to the Templates folder.

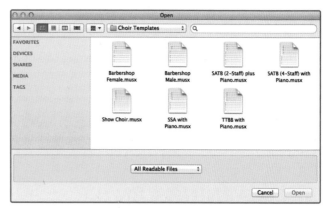

Above: The Templates dialog contains a huge number of ready-made templates for a wide range of styles and ensembles.

EXERCISE WIZARD

The Exercise Wizard is a great way for teachers to create exercises for their pupils, by combining scales, arpeggios and other sequences for practice into one custom document.

SCANNING

Finale comes with a built-in module for 'reading' a scanned sheet of music. Results can vary, depending on the quality of the original scan. You'll almost certainly have to do some checking and editing afterwards.

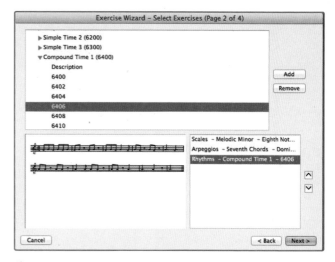

Above: Music teachers can use the Exercise Wizard to create lessons or exercises for their pupils.

OPEN

You can open existing documents by clicking on this button. There's also a drop-down list of Recent Files that you've been working on.

IMPORT MUSICXML

Finale also imports and exports music files as MusicXML. A lot of other music apps have the same capability, which makes transferring files from one app to another very easy.

What is MusicXML?

MusicXML is a format for exchanging data between music apps. You can export a file from Sibelius as MusicXML and then import it into Finale, for example.

LEARNING CENTER

Finale comes with some very extensive Help documentation, which you can access from here. There are also QuickStart Videos that guide you through some of the basics, and a Tip of the Day.

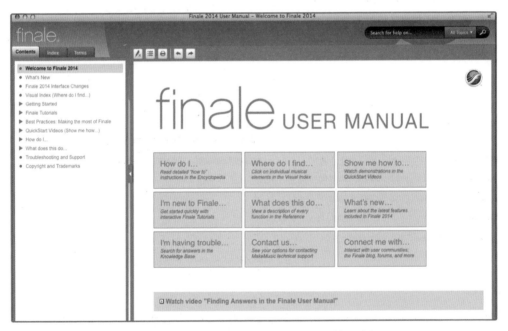

Above: Watch the videos, do the tutorials and read the help pages, to get to grips with Finale's capabilities.

SETUP WIZARD

The easiest way to set up a new document is with the Setup Wizard. You can select it from the Launch Window, or from the File menu (New > Document with Setup Wizard). There are four dialog boxes to work through.

SELECT AN ENSEMBLE AND DOCUMENT STYLE

An ensemble is the group of instruments that you want in your score: a string quartet, a full orchestra, or a four-part choir. If what you want isn't in the list, you can create it in the next pane. Just leave 'Create New Ensemble' selected. A Document Style is the basic settings on which your document is based. You can create your own Document Styles and put them in the Document Styles folder and they will appear in this list in the Setup Wizard.

Top Right: The first dialog box of the Setup Wizard enables you to create the document style of your choice; this is the Mac OS version.

Right: The Windows version of the same dialog box.

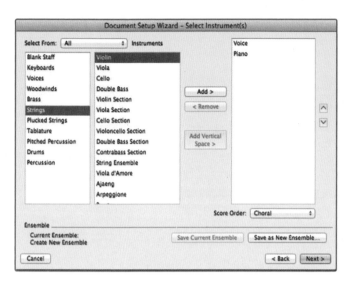

Above: Use the second dialog box of the Setup Wizard to select the instruments of your choice; Mac version.

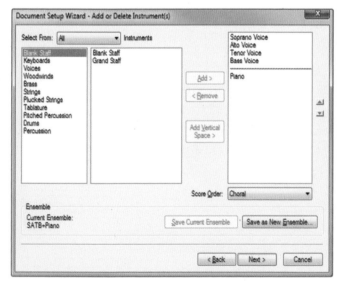

Above: The Windows version of the second dialog box.

SELECT INSTRUMENTS

If you selected an ensemble in the previous pane, its instruments will be listed here. Otherwise, you can start adding instruments to your score. You can modify the list, removing or adding instruments. Finale will automatically place your instruments in the correct order, according to Orchestral, Choral, Concert Band, Marching Band or Jazz Band conventions, using the drop-down list. There is also a Custom option in case you want something different.

You can save your ensemble, and it will appear in the previous dialog box for next time. If you've modified an existing ensemble, you can save your changes for future documents, or keep things as they are.

SCORE INFORMATION

Here's where you enter the title, name of the composer, copyright information and any other information that you want to appear in your score, or just keep for your own information. The contents of these fields can be inserted into text boxes throughout the score, making it easy to add the title as a header on every page, for example.

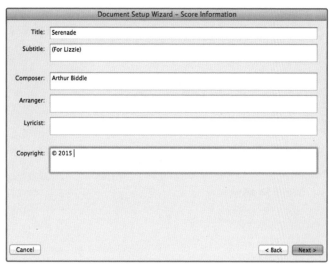

Above: The Score Information dialog box allows you to enter details about the score, such as the date of composition; Mac version.

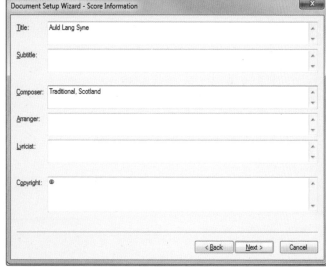

Above: The Windows version of the Score Information dialog box.

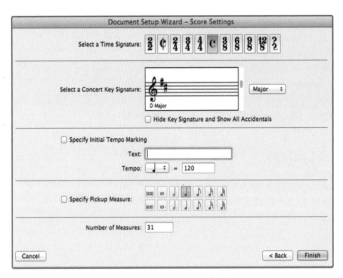

Above: Enter details about the score in the fourth dialog box of the Setup Wizard; Mac version.

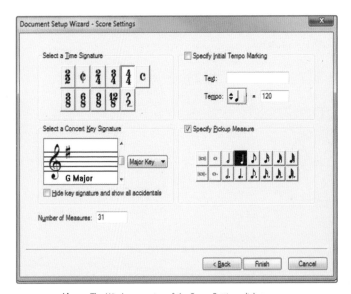

Above: The Windows version of the Score Settings dialog.

SCORE SETTINGS

This is where you enter the time signature, key signature, an initial tempo instruction and beats-per-minute value. You can also define a pick-up measure at the start, and how many bars (measures) you want in the document. Click on Finish, and you're ready to start!

APPLICATION OVERVIEW

Once you've opened a document, you'll see a document window, a menu bar, two or more tool palettes, and the playback controls. If any of these are missing, you can reveal them via the Window menu.

TOOLS

Finale has 29 different tools, and the program works in different ways, depending on which one is selected. There are tools for Staves, Clefs, Text, Chords, Lyrics, Note Entry, Repeats, Page Layout and more. The tool palette can be rearranged to suit your working habits. You'll spend a lot of your time in Finale switching between tools. It is possible to assign keyboard shortcuts to them.

COLOURS

Finale displays some items of your score in different colours. This provides additional information about what type of object it is.

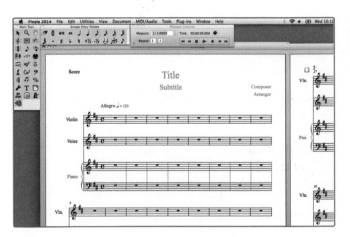

Top right: A typical Finale screen on a Mac.
Right: The Windows version of a typical Finale screen.

Expressions are green, Repeat Marks are blue, Smart Shapes are red. Each of the Layers is a different colour. Scores will normally print in solid black, though there is an option to print the colours.

Instrument Range

Finale will display notes that are impossible or difficult to play in each instrument by using yellow notes. This can be turned on or off in View menu > Out of Range Notes, where different skill levels (Beginner, Intermediate and Advanced) can be set.

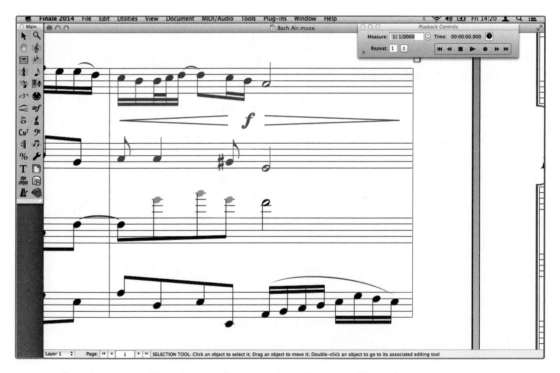

Above: A score showing different Layers, out-of-range notes, slurs and dynamics in different colours.

VIEWS

Finale has two main views: Scroll View and Page View.

Scroll View

Scroll View presents your music on a continuous line, without
any regard for how the music will be divided into systems when
placed on a page. This is very useful when you are entering your
music, before you start to worry about layout.

Page View

Page View presents your music laid out on to pages, and is the WYSIWYG part of Finale. There
are a number of different View Styles, which can be selected from View > Page View Style.

> **Hot Tip**
>
> You can set your
> preferred choice of
> View Style for all newly
> opened documents in
> Preferences > New.

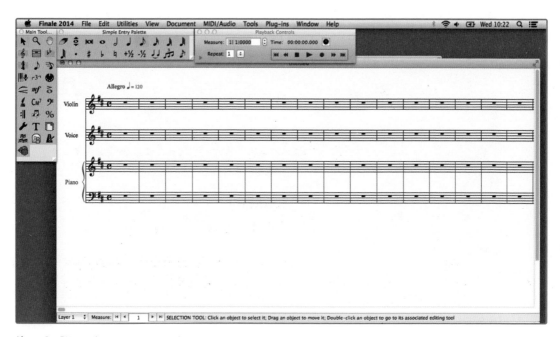

Above: Scroll View is the easiest one to use when you are inputting your music.

LAYERS

In Finale, each staff can contain four independent lines of music. These are called Layers, and it's easy to move between them from the View menu > Select Layer, or from the small control at the bottom left of the document window. Notes in each Layer display in a different colour, so you can easily identify them.

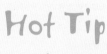

Hot Tip

Always make sure you're using the right Layer!

If you need to move or copy music between Layers, you can do this with 'Move/Copy Layers' in the Edit menu. You can also view only the current layer with 'Show Active Layer Only' in the Document menu.

Below: A Finale document, showing Layers highlighted in different colours.

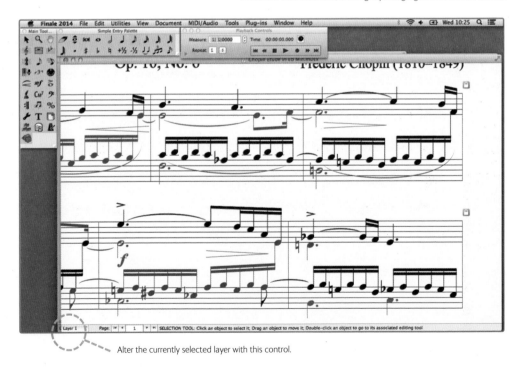

Alter the currently selected layer with this control.

LINKED PARTS

Most instrumentalists perform from a printed 'part' that just contains their staff. They don't need everyone else's notes! One Finale document can contain both a score *and* all the individual parts. The parts are said to be linked, as a change to the score will affect the copy in the parts. Many Finale functions will ask if a change should be applied to the current part, the score, or all the parts and the score. Some elements can be unlinked, so that changes made to the score no longer affect the parts. You can move between the parts and the score in the Document menu (Edit Score/Edit Parts).

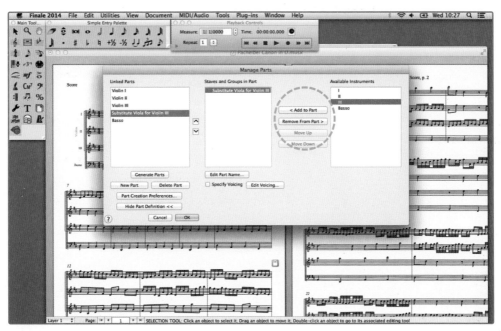

Above: Use the Manage Parts dialog box to add, remove or customize parts.

SAVING YOUR SCORE

The next thing to do with your brand new document is to save it! Saving your document when you start and as you work on it is good practice for any application, in case of any unexpected computer problems. Finale documents have a .musx file extension.

Backup and Auto-Save

Finale also saves a backup copy of your document, either to a backup folder that you select in the app's Preferences > Folders, or to the same folder as the original document. Finale backup files have a .bak file extension. Finale can be set to automatically save the document at set time intervals (Preferences > Save and Print).

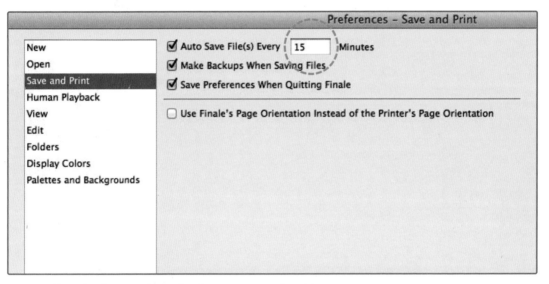

Above: Auto-Save is a good option if you forget to save your work regularly.

NAVIGATING THROUGH YOUR SCORE

There are several different ways to move around your document, using the mouse or keyboard:

- **Scroll**: You can scroll normally through the window using a mouse scroll wheel or a trackpad.

- **Page Controls**: You can use the Page Controls at the bottom of the document window to move through each page.

- **Hand Grabber Tool**: The Hand Grabber Tool lets you click and 'grab' the document to move it about. A shortcut for the Hand Grabber is right-click (PC) and Command + Alt + click (Mac).

- **Keys**: You can also use the Home, End, Page Up and Page Down keys to navigate. In Page View, holding Ctrl (PC) or Command (Mac) with the Page Up/Down keys will move you through pages.

Hand Grabber Tool

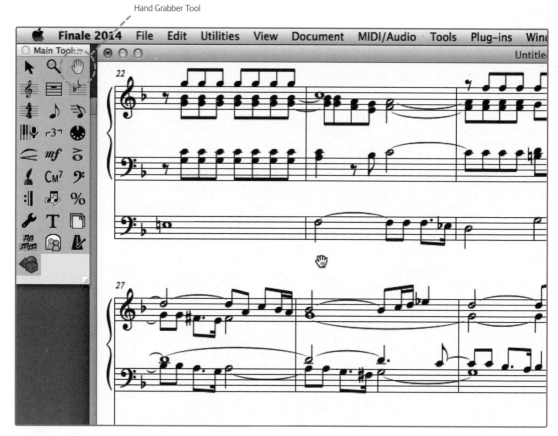

Above: The Hand Grabber Tool is a faster, more efficient way of moving around the score than using the scroll bars.

NOTE ENTRY

NOTE ENTRY

Finale has three separate tools for entering notes – HyperScribe, Speedy Entry and Simple Entry – and each of them supports different methods getting your music on the page.

OVERVIEW

Three separate tools for note entry, each with their own methods, settings and keyboard shortcuts, can seem like a lot to take in. There is no real need to learn all three; many professional users of Finale with years of experience will never use more than one of them.

HyperScribe

HyperScribe involves using a MIDI instrument to play notes into the computer using a beat from Finale. It will be described in full later in this chapter.

Speedy Entry and Simple Entry

Speedy Entry and Simple Entry have a number of similarities.

Hot Tip

When using the Selection Tool, double-clicking on a note will activate the Simple Entry Tool.

Both of them can be used to enter notes, either with just the computer keyboard, or with the computer keyboard and a MIDI instrument together. In this book, we are going to focus on Simple Entry, which is perhaps the more comprehensive of the entry methods. There is nothing 'speedier' about Speedy Entry – you can enter music just as quickly with Simple Entry – and Simple Entry has a couple of features that aren't in Speedy.

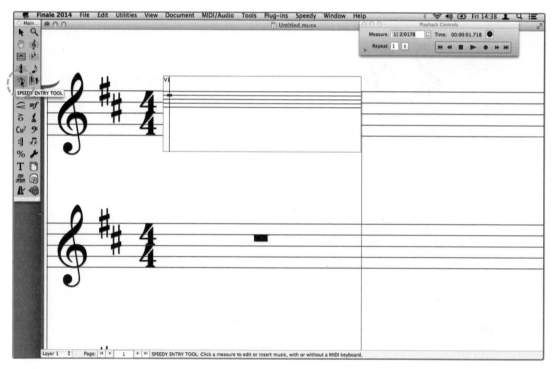

Above: Speedy Entry is one of three ways of entering notes into Finale.

SIMPLE ENTRY

Simple Entry is the easiest and most complete of the entry methods. You can enter notes directly with the mouse, with your computer keyboard, or with a MIDI instrument. It is also the most useful for editing an existing score.

Simple Entry Tool

Above: Clicking on the Simple Entry Tool will display the caret – equivalent to the cursor in a word-processing program – which you will use to enter your music.

SELECTING THE TOOL

You can select Simple Entry from the Tools menu in the menu bar or from the Main Tool Palette. The Simple Entry Palette should appear, if it's not already there, showing 20 musical symbols. There's also a palette with rest symbols on it.

Hot Tip

Using the Selection Tool, double-clicking on any note will select Simple Entry.

THE CARET

At the start of the score, you will see a vertical purple line with a quaver note symbol in the middle of it. This is the Simple Entry Caret, the equivalent of the caret (or cursor) that you see in a word processor as you type a line of text. The quaver note will be on the middle line of the staff. If you move your mouse around, you will see that the pointer on the screen is also a quaver note. You can use the mouse to place the note in any position and click notes into place. You can click on an icon in the Simple Entry Palette to change the note value.

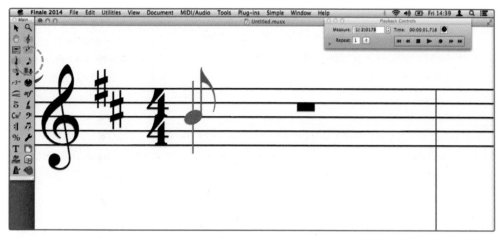

Above: In Finale's Simple Entry mode, the caret is your friend.

KEYBOARD ENTRY

Some people find using the mouse to enter notes a bit slow and fiddly. It is possible to use the keyboard instead.

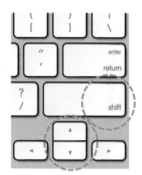

○ **Up and down arrow keys:**
These keys move the note in the caret to any position on the staff:

Hot Tip

Holding Shift with the up/down arrows will move the caret by one octave.

- **Return:** Press Return to enter a note at that pitch.
- **Shift + Return:** Pressing Shift + Return will enter a rest of the same value.
- **Note names:** Alternatively, you can type the name of the note (A–G) to enter the note.

When typing pitches with the keyboard, the note will be entered at the octave closest to the caret's position.

CHANGING NOTE VALUES

Finale has many keyboard commands that can really speed up your workflow. To change note values, use keys 1 to 8 on the number pad.

Hot Tip

If you enter the wrong note, just press Delete, as you would when typing text.

No Number Pad?

If your keyboard doesn't have a number pad, you can alter the shortcut assignments in Simple Entry menu > Simple Entry Options > Edit Shortcuts. There's a built-in set for laptops that don't have a number pad. You can see all the currently assigned shortcuts in the Simple Entry Command menu. To enter a rest, press 0 on the number pad.

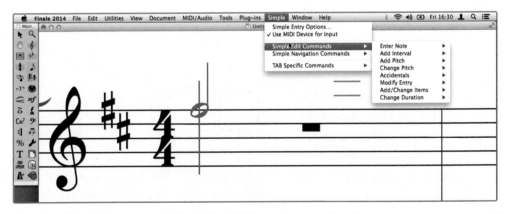

Above: To modify anything on your score, head to the Simple Edit Commands menu, as pictured here.

USING MIDI ENTRY

If you have a MIDI instrument attached to your computer, you can use it to enter pitches. You still have to specify your note value with your computer keyboard, but any note you play will be entered into the score. This makes adding chords or long runs of notes easy. Make sure that 'Use MIDI Device for Input' is selected in the Simple Entry menu. You can turn this off if you want to play the keyboard without adding notes to your score.

No MIDI Instrument?

Don't worry if you haven't got a MIDI instrument. Finale makes it easy to build chords or play in long sequences using just your computer keyboard.

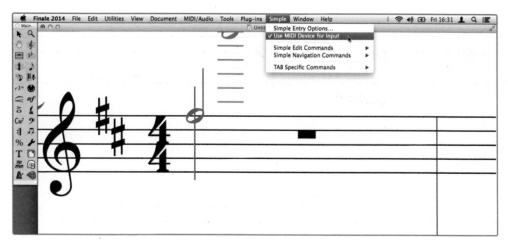

Above: Using MIDI entry makes adding more complex passages of music much easier.

ADDING ELEMENTS WITH THE KEYBOARD

You can also add elements to the currently selected note using the keyboard. Press the full-stop key to add a dot to the note. Press T to add a tie. R will turn the current note into a rest. Pressing + or - will add a sharp or a flat respectively. You can also enter commands from the Simple Entry menu.

ADDING ELEMENTS FROM THE PALETTE

The Simple Entry Palette has several other icons that 'augment' the note, such as a tie, a dot, a grace note or an accidental. These icons are selected in addition to note values and they affect all new notes. Click the icon again to deselect it.

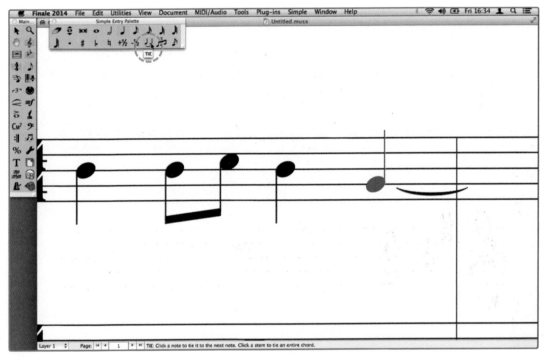

Above: Use the icons on the Simple Entry Palette to enter items such as ties, as shown here.

BUILDING CHORDS

You can also add notes to build a chord. On the main keyboard, numbers 2 to 8 correspond to the interval above the note. Hold down Shift to add notes below the current note. If you're using the laptop shortcut set, the F keys do the same thing. You can check in the Simple Entry menu which shortcut set you're using, and what each command's shortcut is.

TRIPLETS

You can create a simple triplet by selecting a note value and the triplet icon in the Simple Entry Palette. When you enter the note, a triplet will be created (three of the current note value), or you can press 9 on the keypad after entering the first note.

Hot Tip

If you need a more complex rhythm, like a quintuplet, press Alt 9 to change the definition of the tuplet.

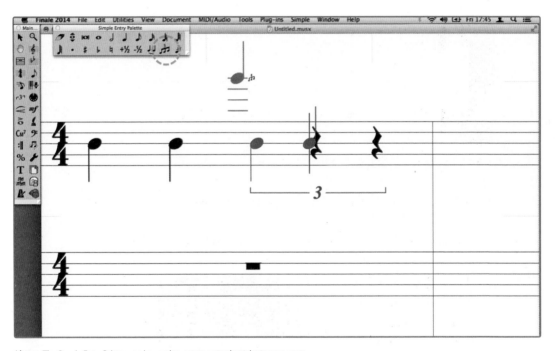

Above: The Simple Entry Palette can be used to create a simple triplet in your score.

NAVIGATING IN SIMPLE ENTRY

Working in Simple Entry, you'll want to move around the score. Here are some ways to navigate:

1. You can click with the mouse in any measure (bar) to start entering notes there.

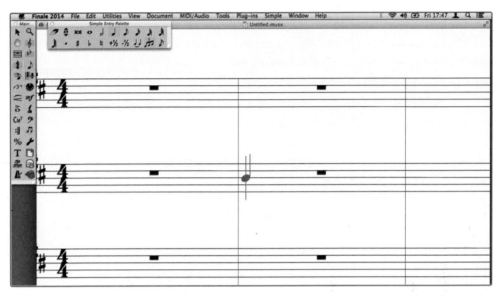

Above: To move to another staff using the keyboard, press Ctrl + up or down arrow.

2. You can use the arrow keys to move backwards or forwards through the notes.

3. The up and down arrow keys will move the selected note on the staff.

4. If you want to move up through a chord (or on to the next staff), use Command + up/down (Mac) or Ctrl + up/down (PC).

5. Pressing Command (Mac) or Ctrl (PC) + left/right arrows moves the caret by one whole measure.

Hot Tip

Pressing the right arrow key in a half-filled measure will fill it with any rests that are needed.

ADVANCED SIMPLE ENTRY

We've covered the basics of Simple Entry, but there's much more that can be done. You can change the Clef, Key and Time Signature without having to leave the Simple Entry Tool. Just type Alt + C for Clef, Alt + T for Time or Alt + K for Key. (It's the same on Mac and PC.) Then select a clef, time or key from the dialog, or use one of Finale's many shortcuts to access the most common choices.

More Shortcuts

Articulations can be added to notes in the same way. Just press * on the number pad and then type the articulation's shortcut, or choose one from the Selection dialog. Expressions, too, can be added by pressing X.

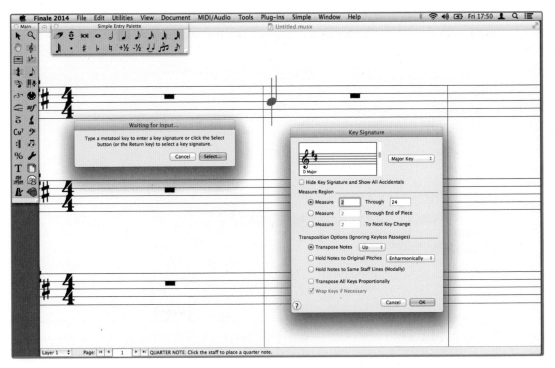

Above: Pressing Alt + K brings up the Key Signature dialog box in Simple Entry.

PERCUSSION

Percussion can call for a slightly different type of notation from other instruments. Sometimes, a staff will only display one pitch, as the instrument has only one tone. Sometimes, different pitches on a percussion staff will represent different instruments. Whatever you need, Finale has a way to display it.

OVERVIEW

If you plan to use percussion staves in your score, then you need to select the correct type of percussion staff from the Setup Wizard when you create your document. Finale has a range of different staves for individual instruments and percussion groups.

Above: Select the percussion instrument of your choice using the Setup Wizard.

Percussion Staves

There are three types of percussion staff: Pitched Percussion, Single-Line and Five-Line. Pitched Percussion staves are no different from normal staves, for instruments like a xylophone. Single-line staves are for individual instruments that have one pitch, like a triangle or snare drum. Five-line staves are for percussion staves that notate more than one instrument.

> **Hot Tip**
>
> Make sure you've got the right instrument setup for the percussion that you want.

Note Entry

Finale uses the Simple Entry Tool to enter percussion notes, in a similar way to standard staves. Next to the caret, you will see the name of a percussion instrument or technique. Using the up and down arrows, move through the list until you get to the instrument you want, then enter the note.

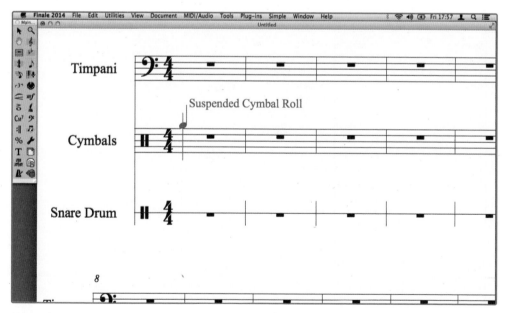

Above: When you enter a percussion note, the name of the instrument will appear next to it.

TABLATURE

Tablature ('tab') notation is a representation of finger patterns for fretboards on guitars and other instruments. Finale uses a modified staff and special mode in Simple Entry for creating tablature.

OVERVIEW

Finale uses a modified mode of Simple Entry, with different keyboard shortcuts, for entering tablature. Instead of notes, tablature has numbers representing the finger positions on the fretboard. These are placed on each line of the staff, which represents the instrument's strings.

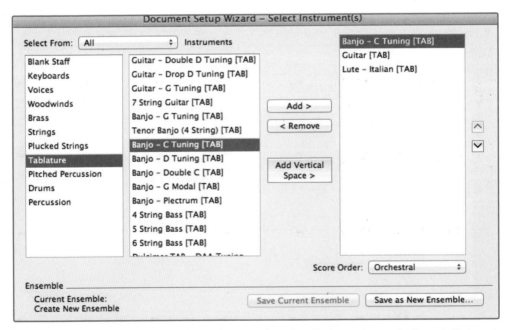

Above: This Setup Wizard shows the different tablature styles you can choose from. Use the arrow keys to select the required instrument.

As with other instrument types, the first step is choosing an instrument in the Setup Wizard. There are several tablature styles for different instruments, such as Guitar, Banjo and Lute. Different string tunings are also provided.

TAB ENTRY

Entering tab notation can be confusing at first, but there are a few simple rules that will help:

1. Click on a string. This will place a 0 (zero) on the string.

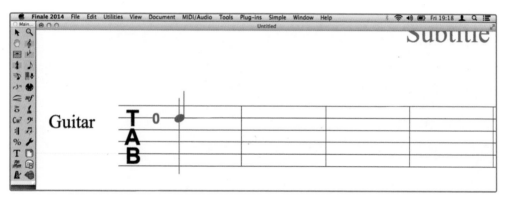

Step 1: Clicking on a string will automatically place a 0 on the string.

2. Change the fret number using the number pad.

3. Add strings to the chord by clicking on other strings in the same position.

> **Hot Tip**
>
> If you need to type '11' or another double-digit number, just type them quickly.

Keyboard Shortcuts

Like standard Simple Entry, Tab Entry has a lot of keyboard shortcuts that can save you time. There is a set for shorter laptop keyboards and full desktop keyboards. Look at 'Tab Specific Commands' in the Simple Entry menu.

Copying Notes

Another way to get Tablature notation into your score is to enter the music on a standard notation staff and then copy and paste it to a tab staff.

1. Using the Selection Tool, select the measures (bars) that you want to copy in the standard staff.

2. Next, copy the measures (Command + C [Mac], Ctrl + C [PC]).

3. Select the first measure in your tab staff and paste (Command + V [Mac], Ctrl + V [PC]).

4. Finale will automatically enter the notes using the lowest strings possible, or you can specify the lowest string to use. Using the Selection Tool will be explored further in the chapter Editing Your Score, pages 80–98.

Hot Tip

Alt-click in a score to paste the currently selected measures to a new location.

Above: Create TAB notation by copying existing notes and pasting them into a tab staff.

HYPERSCRIBE

Finale's built-in method transcribing notes directly from a MIDI instrument is called HyperScribe. It has its own tool in the Main Tools Palette.

OVERVIEW

In order for HyperScribe to interpret your playing correctly, it needs a reference beat. This can be created in one of three ways, each of which is shown under the Beat Source sub-menu of HyperScribe's menu. First, Finale can supply the beat itself, either from playing the music already in the document, or from a click. The second option is for the click to come from your external MIDI hardware. The third option is for you to supply the click yourself.

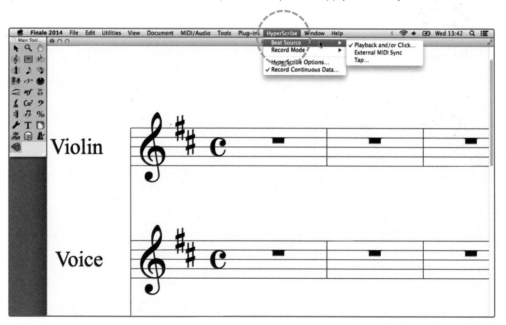

Above: Choose Playback and/or Click if you want Finale to supply a metronome click for the beat.

Playback and Click

By default, Finale will play back existing music in the score and provide a click for you to play along with. You can use the playback controls to set the tempo, and to start the recording by pressing the 'Record' button. If you want to change the type of click, the trigger to start recording, or use a different tempo for recording, then these can all be configured in the Playback and/or Click dialog.

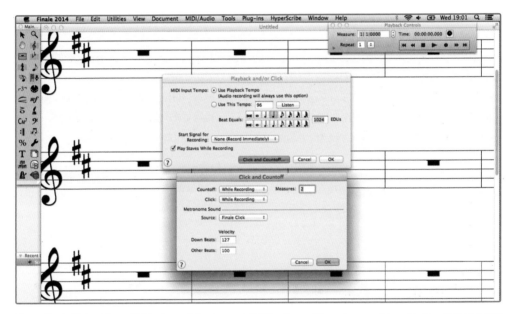

Above: Use the Click and Countoff dialog box to define the countoff click settings and the metronome click used for HyperScribe recording.

External MIDI Beat

If you want to provide a beat or tempo from an external MIDI source, then choose 'External MIDI Sync' from the Beat Source sub-menu. You'll need the right MIDI hardware to do this.

Tap

You can provide your own beat (a 'Tap') for Finale, using a MIDI controller such as a sustain pedal, or a button on your keyboard, or even a note. The advantage of this method is that your taps do not have to be even. Finale will divide all the notes played between the taps as fractions of the duration between two taps. So, if your tap represents a crotchet, and you play two equal notes between taps, then they will be entered as quavers, regardless of how fast or irregular your taps are.

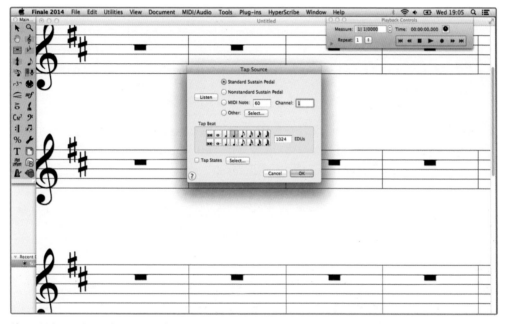

Above: It's best to choose the Tap option if you're going to be tapping a pedal or a key while you play.

Quantization

Humans tend to play music in a way that computers find imprecise. If you're a millisecond off the beat, then how should Finale notate this? Quantization defines the shortest note value that Finale should work to. Finale will try to 'fit' the notes that you play to the nearest quantization value. Select 'Quantization Settings' from the MIDI/Audio menu.

The Best Results

Even with optimal settings, you need to play strictly in time and without overlapping notes. You'll almost certainly have to do some work in Simple Entry afterwards.

Starting to Play

Once you've got all the many settings exactly as you want them, then you're ready to play the music.

1. You can either click into a specific measure and start from there, or press 'Record' on the playback controls.

2. You'll see a grey box that outlines the measure and hear the count-off click. By default, there is a two bar count-off before the recording starts. This lets you get used to the tempo and gives you time to get to the instrument!

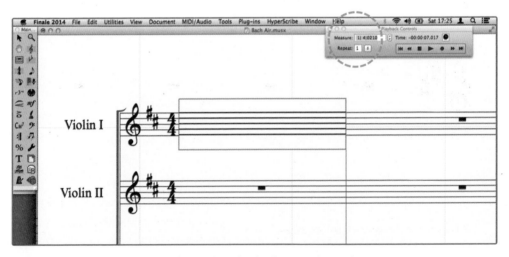

Above: Click a measure to start recording using HyperScribe, and Finale will start recording into that measure.

3. Play your music! Finale shows the results after each measure (bar) is completed. By default, HyperScribe treats each measure as a separate rhythm, so tied notes must be played twice.

Other HyperScribe Options

HyperScribe can also record two lines of music played at the same time, using a 'split point' on the MIDI keyboard to divide the notes into two staves. It's also possible to Multitrack Record into several staves at once. In this mode, you can enter 16 MIDI channels into Finale all at once. This is only possible with certain types of MIDI equipment. These options can be set in the HyperScribe menu's Record Mode sub-menu.

Another command in the menu, 'Record Continuous Data', allows the transcription of underlying MIDI data, other than notes. This can include Pitch Bend, Modulation and any other data that your MIDI instrument can generate.

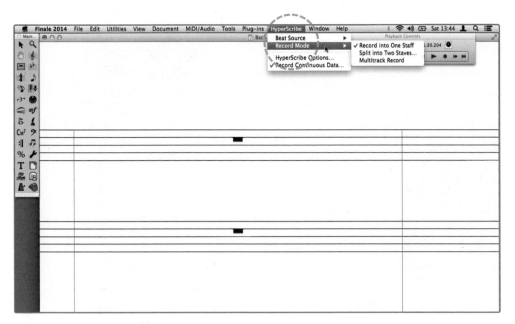

Above: Choose this Record Mode command to notate your performance on to one staff.

ADDING DETAIL TO YOUR SCORE

ADDING DETAIL TO YOUR SCORE

Music notation isn't just notes, of course. There are plenty of other elements in a score, like articulations, expressions, lyrics, chords and shapes, including slurs and hairpins. There can be blocks of text and graphics. Finale has a range of tools to do all this.

ARTICULATIONS

Articulations are symbols that attach to a note, such as accents, trills and fermatas, and marks to indicate staccato, tenuto and marcato. Finale's default documents come with all these articulations built in, but it's also very easy to make your own. To add, edit and create articulations, you need to select the Articulation Tool.

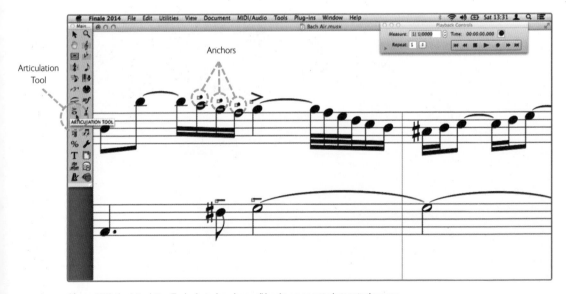

Above: With the Articulation Tool selected, anchors will be shown on articulations in the score.

Hot Tip

The shortcut for each articulation is shown in the top right-hand corner of each articulation in the Selection dialog.

Anchor Points

As soon as you select the Articulation Tool, any articulations in your score will show a small, transparent rectangle next to them, called 'anchor points'. Using the anchor point, you can select the articulation to edit, delete or move it. You can move the articulation with the mouse or by 'nudging' with the arrow keys.

Adding an Articulation

There are two ways to add an articulation. Either double-click on the note and select the articulation from the selection dialog, or hold down the shortcut key for the articulation you want, and click on the note.

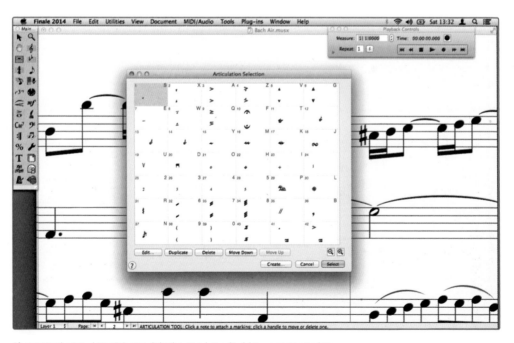

Above: Use the Articulation Selection dialog box to select, edit, delete or create articulations.

LYRICS

No song is complete without lyrics! Finale has a tool just for lyrics, and it has some powerful features and capabilities. Click on the Lyric Tool to get started.

TYPE INTO SCORE

The Lyric Tool has several different modes, and the default is 'Type Into Score'. As the name suggests, all you have to do is click on a note, and then you can type the lyrics directly into the score. Typing a hyphen will take you to the next note, and Finale will space out hyphens between the syllables as needed. Typing a space will also move you to the next note, and Finale will automatically make 'Word Extensions' (lines after a word) as needed.

Above: Type Into Score lets you attach each syllable to any note.

The Lyrics Window

The Lyrics window shows you the syllables you've entered as you type. You can make corrections to the words here. You can also control the lyric category and number, and choose the modes of the Lyric Tool.

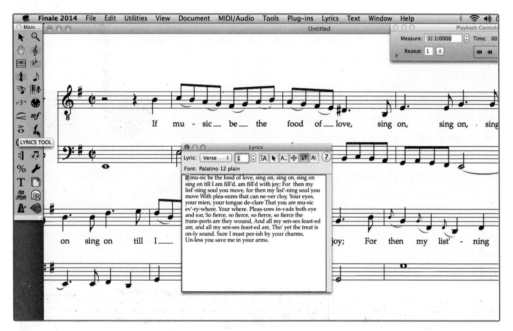

Above: Edit your lyrics in the Lyrics window, as you would do in a word-processing document.

Lyric Categories

Finale categorizes lyrics into three groups: Verse, Chorus and Section. There's no real difference between them; it's purely for your own organization. Lyrics can also be in a number group, so Verse 1, 2, 3 ..., Chorus 1, 2, 3 ... and so on to 4095! Press the down arrow while typing in the score to move to the next lyric number.

Hot Tip

Turn on 'Auto-number' in the Lyrics menu to display the verse number at the start of the lyrics.

Four Arrows

When you use the Type Into Score mode, you'll see four arrows at the side of the staff, which control the position of lyrics. From the left: the first arrow sets the baseline for that lyric group and number (for example, Verse 1) on every staff throughout the score; the next one sets the baseline only for that staff, throughout the piece; the third arrow sets the baseline for that staff, just on that system; and the last one sets the baseline for the next syllable that you enter.

You can also set baselines with numerical values from the 'Adjust Baselines' command in the Lyrics menu. Similar arrows are used in other tools.

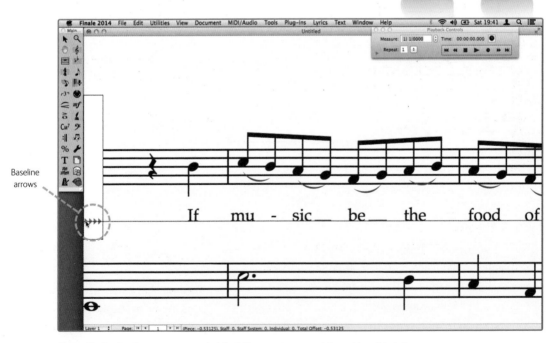

Baseline arrows

Above: The four baseline arrows, seen to the left of this screenshot, control the position of the lyrics.

CLICK ASSIGNMENT

This is another mode of the Lyric Tool, accessed from the Lyrics menu or the icons in the Lyrics window. Instead of typing directly into the score, you type all the hyphenated syllables into the Lyrics window, then you click each syllable on to the relevant note. Holding Alt while clicking will fill all the lyrics into consecutive notes.

Hot Tip

Use a decent hyphenation dictionary that shows you how to split your lyric syllables correctly.

WORD EXTENSIONS

Go to Lyrics > Edit Word Extensions, and you will be able to edit word extensions (the lines that appear after a word when it is sung to more than one note).

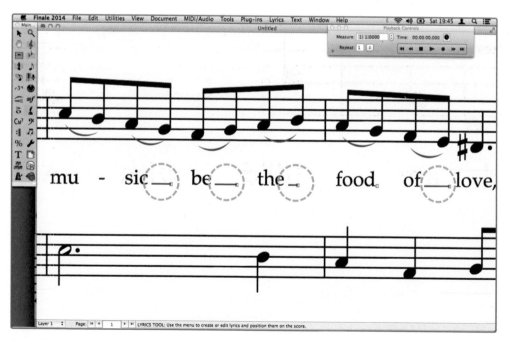

Above: To edit a word extension, click near the syllable to be extended; a handle (or anchor point) will appear at the end of the syllable.

SHIFT LYRICS

If you've entered your music, but forgotten to leave a gap for a melisma, don't worry. You can use the Shift Lyrics mode to move the lyrics to the right (or to the left, if you've left too much room!). When you select this mode, there is a dialog to set which way you want to move the lyrics and the method by which you want them to move., then just click on the note where the lyrics need to move to.

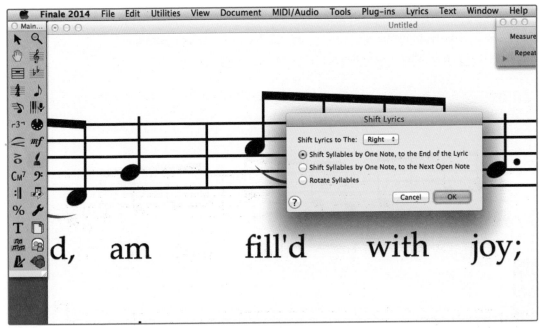

Above: The Shift Lyrics dialog box allows you to move lyrics as you wish.

ADJUST SYLLABLES

This mode displays an anchor point next to every syllable, so that you can adjust the position for fine-tuning of your lyrics.

EXPRESSIONS

Finale uses the Expression Tool to control various symbols, words and sentences that are attached to the music. These include Dynamics, Tempo Marks, Rehearsal Marks and other instructions. Each of these types is dealt with as a different 'category', whose behaviour and appearance can be defined separately.

Above: Finale's Expression Tool.

OVERVIEW

The Expression Tool is similar to the Articulation Tool: double-click on a note and select an expression from the Selection dialog, or hold down the keyboard shortcut and click. The numbers 1 to 0 are the shortcuts for the dynamic symbols, ffff to pppp, while R is for *ritardando* and T for a *tempo*.

Right: In this piece of music, the forte (f) sign is marked in green. In Finale, all expressions, such as Tempo Marks and dynamics, are displayed in green.

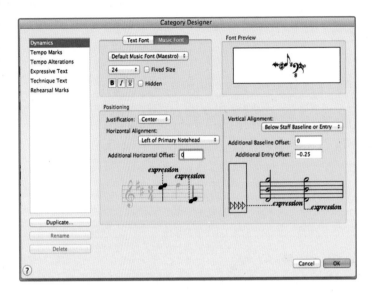

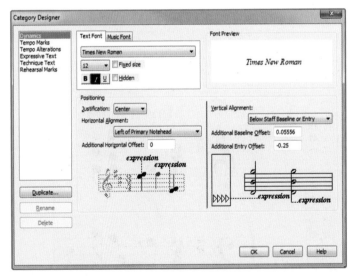

Above: With the Category Designer, you can give each category of expressions (such as Dynamics or Tempo Marks) its own characteristics. (**Top:** the Mac window; **Bottom:** the Windows window)

CATEGORIES

Finale divides expressions into Dynamics, Tempo Marks, Tempo Alterations, Expressive Marks, Technique Marks, Rehearsal Marks and Miscellaneous. All but the last of these can be configured using the Category Designer (Document menu), where you can set the font, size and position of expressions in each group. You can also control playback effects, so that your Tempo Marks change the tempo when you play the score. You can also create your own categories if you need more. Expressions in the 'Miscellaneous' category are defined individually and are not controlled by the Category Designer.

Hot Tip

To make them clear, all expressions display in green on your document, but they print in black!

Score Lists

Three of the existing categories (Tempo Marks, Tempo Alterations and Rehearsal Marks) use 'Score Lists'. By editing the checkboxes in the Score List, you can decide which staves in your score will show the expression. For instance, it's common to show Tempo Marks above each instrumental group in an orchestral score, or only on the very top staff of a choral score. There are eight separate Score Lists you can use.

Rehearsal Marks

Hold M and click in the score to add a Rehearsal Mark. The letter symbol will automatically increase every time it appears in the score.

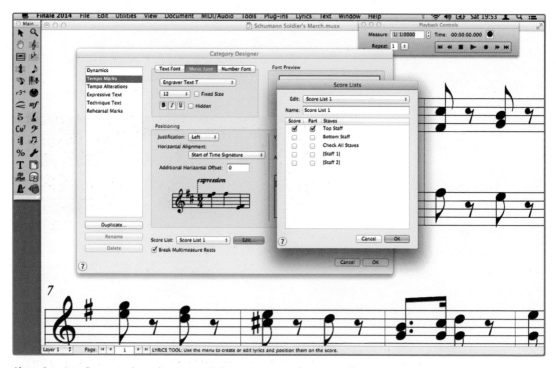

Above: Score Lists allow you to choose the staves on which certain categories of expression will appear.

SLURS, HAIRPINS AND OTHER SHAPES

Finale has different tools for dealing with a range of lines and curves that you can add to the score. This includes slurs, hairpins, brackets, glissandi, slides, trills and octave markings. In Finale, these symbols are called Smart Shapes.

Above: Finale's Smart Shape Palette.

THE SMART SHAPE PALETTE

All the Smart Shapes are shown in the Smart Shape Palette. This appears when you select any of the Shape tools from the Tool menu, or you can reveal it using the Window menu.

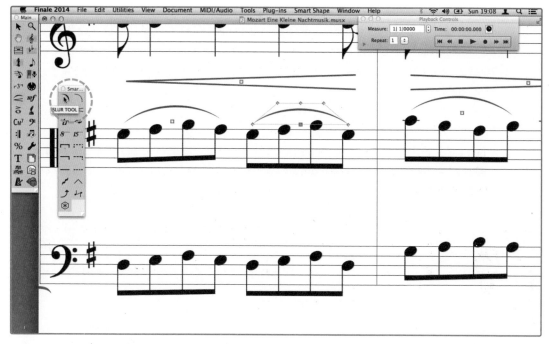

Above: The Smart Shape Tool helps you add slurs and hairpins to your score.

Switching Shapes

When you've selected one Smart Shape tool, you can create any Smart Shape by holding down a shortcut key while you click: S for slur, comma for crescendo, full stop for decrescendo, T for trill.

SLURS

With the Slur Tool selected, you can draw slurs between notes. A double-click on a note will create a slur to the next note. For longer slurs, you need to double-click and drag. This can take a bit of practice. Alternatively, create a simple slur with a double-click and then edit it.

Editing the Slur

When using any of the Shape tools, you will see an anchor point on every shape. Click once on a slur's anchor point to reveal more anchors. You can drag these to adjust the shape or length of the slur.

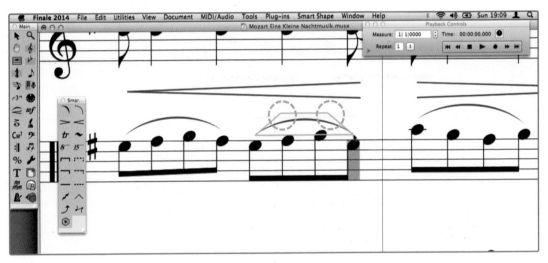

Above: To adjust the length of a slur, click on the appropriate anchor point and then drag to shorten (or lengthen) it, as required.

HAIRPINS

Hairpins are created by a double-click and drag. As with slurs, once you've created the hairpin, you can edit it to make it longer at either end or make the mouth wider. Click once on the main anchor point to show the editing anchor points.

Aligning Hairpins

Drag a rectangle to select several hairpins at once. The anchor points will turn pink when selected. Then right-click to bring up a contextual menu. You'll see options to align the hairpins horizontally and vertically.

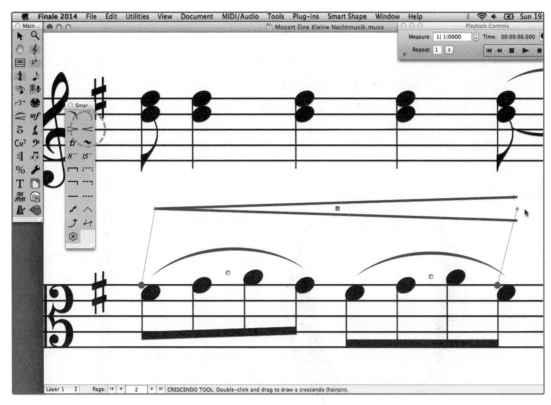

Above: Use the Crescendo/Decrescendo tools in the Smart Shape Palette to insert hairpins; you can then edit and move them at the click of a mouse.

OTHER SHAPES

The other shapes all work in the same way as slurs and hairpins. You can even create your own shapes by Alt-clicking on the Custom Line Tool icon in the Smart Shape Palette.

CHORDS

Finale has a Chord Tool for entering chord symbols on to your score. Chords can be text, such as 'B♭min7/E', and can also include a fretboard diagram.

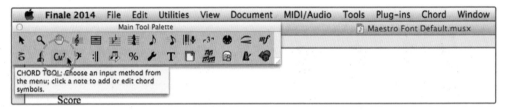

Above: Finale's Chord Tool.

OVERVIEW

Entering chords in Finale is a bit like entering lyrics. Click on a staff with the Chord Tool and you will see a flashing cursor and the four baseline arrows at the side. There are three ways of entering chords: typing the text directly; playing a chord on a MIDI instrument; or having Finale analyse your score. A chord spelling can be made up of three parts: a root (B♭), a suffix (m7) and an alternative bass (F), separated by a forward slash.

Above: Chords can be entered through MIDI; automatically by Finale; or manually, as shown here.

Manual Input

Click on a note, and you'll get a cursor. First, type the root, A to G. Add a sharp with # or a flat with b. You can then add a suffix, like 'maj7(add9)'. If you want to browse Finale's suffix library, type :0 and press Return. You'll then see the complete list of suffixes that Finale knows, and you can select one from

there. Each suffix has a number. Instead of selecting or typing the whole suffix, you can type a colon followed by its number. Type a forward slash and add an alternative bass, if required. Press Space to move to the next note.

Hot Tip

Select 'Show Fretboards' from the Chord menu to add fretboard charts.

Above: Double-click the suffix you want to add to your chord, having first chosen it from the Chord Suffix Selection box.

Chord Entry from MIDI Instrument

If you have a MIDI instrument, select 'Allow MIDI Input' from the Chord menu. Instead of typing in the chord, you can play it, and Finale will interpret the chord and type it into the score. This is the easiest way of adding chords.

Staff Analysis

Another easy way of entering chords is to let Finale analyse one or more staves in your score. Select one of the Staff Analysis modes from the Chord menu (One-Staff, Two-Staff or All-Staff) and then click on a staff. Finale will add the chord based on the notation you've already entered.

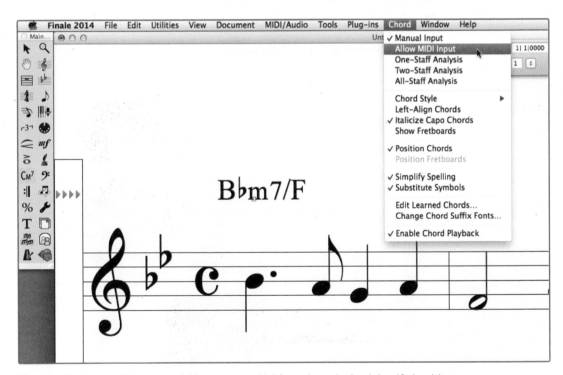

Above: The Chord menu enables you to specify how you want to add, define or change chord symbols and fretboard diagrams.

REPEATS

There are several different kinds of repeat symbols used in music notation, and Finale can produce them all. Although Finale has a dedicated Repeat Tool for the task, most repeats can be created without even using it!

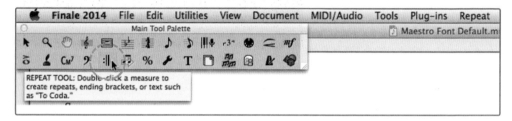

Above: Finale's Repeat Tool.

REPEATS WITH THE SELECTION TOOL

To create a simple repeat, just select the measures (bars) that are to be repeated with the Selection Tool, and right-click to get a contextual menu. Under the Repeats sub-menu, choose 'Create Simple Repeat'. You'll get repeat signs at the start and end of your selected region. Other options are also under this menu.

Hot Tip

To select a region, click on the first measure and then Shift-click on the final measure.

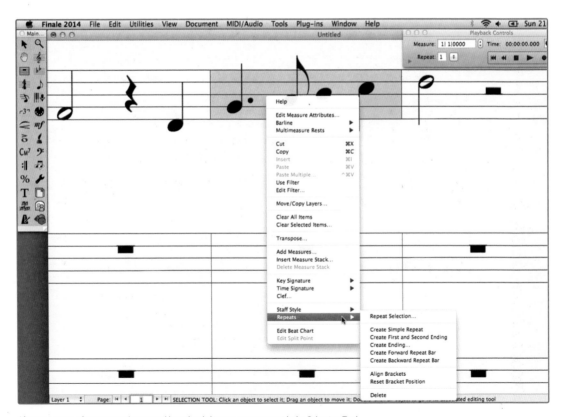

Above: A range of repeats can be created by right-clicking on a measure with the Selection Tool.

Larger Repeat Sections

If your repeat section is very large, you might not want to select the whole region. It might be easier to place the forward repeat and the backward repeat separately. You can do that from the same Repeats sub-menu in the right-click menu of the Selection Tool.

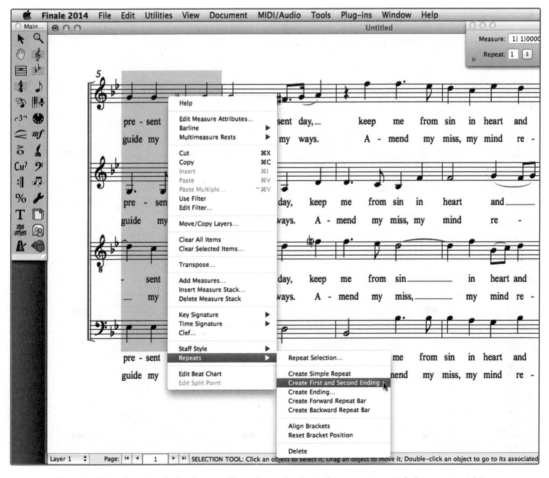

Above: By clicking this option, Finale will create a first and second ending to the repeat, automatically (*see image to right*).

First and Second Endings

You can also use the same process to create first and second endings as for Simple Repeats (above). With the Selection Tool, select the measures for your first ending, and right-click. From the Repeats sub-menu, choose 'Create First and Second endings'. You'll see the repeat signs added to your score.

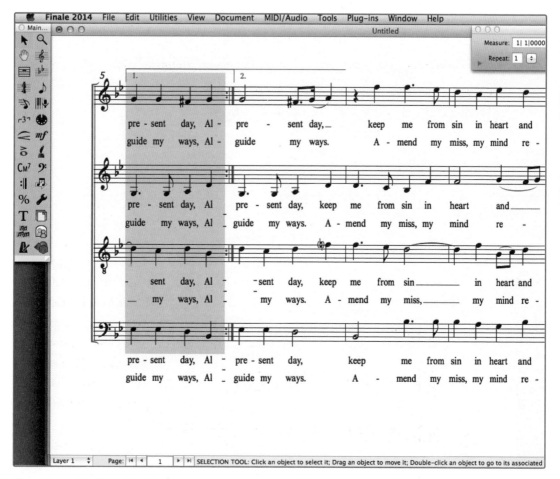

Above: The completed first and second ending.

TEXT BOXES

Finale lets you add text boxes to any part of your score. This can be used for titles, page numbers, or even lengthier prose, like a translation of foreign language lyrics.

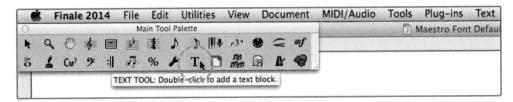

Above: Finale's Text Tool.

Left: By clicking the Assign To Measure option in the drop-down menu, the text you enter will move with a particular measure.

THE TEXT TOOL

As always, Finale has a specific tool for a specific job. With the Text Tool, you can add text that is attached to the music or attached to the page. If the layout of your score changes, then text attached to a measure will move, but text attached to the page will not. The Text menu has options: 'Assign To Measure' or 'Assign To Page'. Text assigned to a measure will appear in red on the screen.

Creating a Text Box

Create a text box by double-clicking on the score with the Text Tool. You'll get a small box with a cursor in it, which will expand as you type. You can alter the shape of the box by dragging from its outline. (The cursor will change shape to an arrow.) To set the shape of the text box when you create the box, double-click and drag to the size you want. Using the Frame Attributes dialog (from the Text menu), you can set what pages the box will display on, and the exact distance from the page or margin edge.

Hot Tip

Check whether text is assigned to measure or page before you create your text box.

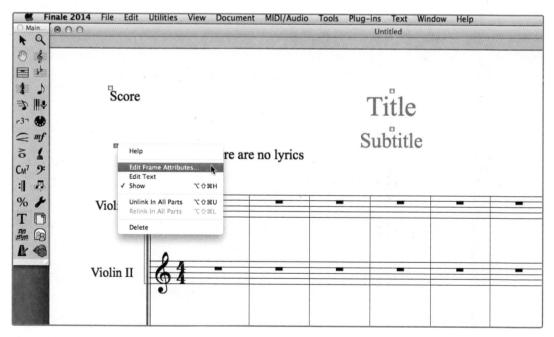

Above: Edit Frame Attributes lets you control; exactly where the text box will appear.

Styling Your Text

The Text menu has many of the commands that you would find in a word processor. You can select the font, size and style. You can alter the alignment and justification. You can add a frame to the box ('Standard Frame' command). You can select a text box for styling by clicking on its anchor point.

Text Inserts

When you created your document, you provided information such as the title, composer and a copyright message. You can insert these fields into a text box with the Insert command in the Text menu. There is other information available too, like page number, current date, and calculated performance time.

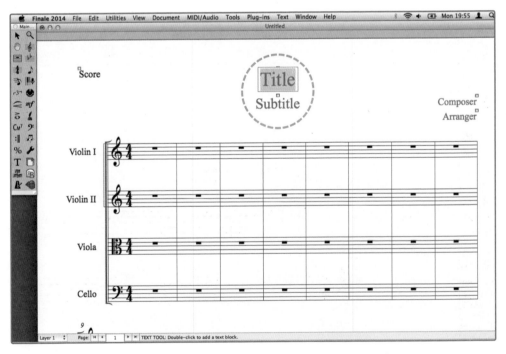

Above: Text fields from the File Info tab of the Score Manager can be used in text boxes, wherever needed.

Page Numbers

You can easily create text fields for page numbers that change position on facing pages. The Frame Attributes dialog has options for left- and right-hand pages, so you can set the same text box to appear in different positions on different pages.

Another useful trick with page numbers is that you can set a 'Page Number Offset'. This is a number that increases the actual page number to a higher value. For instance, you could create three movements of a symphony in separate Finale documents, continuing the page count across all three documents using 'Edit Page Offset' in the Text menu.

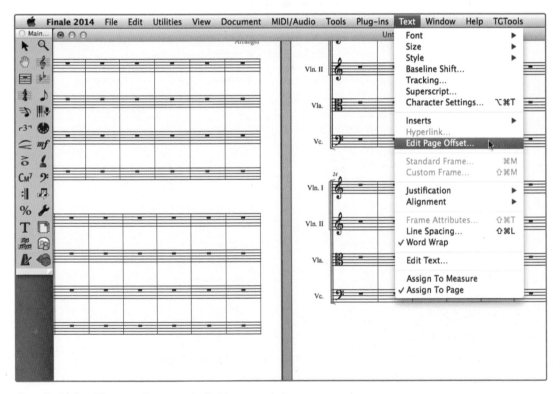

Above: The Edit Page Offset option allows you to alter Finale's current, and subsequent page numbers.

GRAPHICS

In addition to text and music, Finale also lets you add graphics to your page. Finale can import images in GIF, JPEG, TIFF, PNG, PDF and EPS formats. Like text, the graphics can be attached to a measure or page.

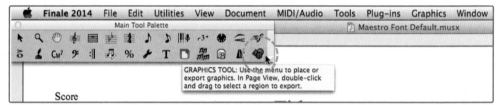

Above: Finale's Graphics Tool.

ADDING A GRAPHIC

Like text boxes, graphics can be assigned to measures or pages. Check the Graphics menu for the assignment that you want. To add a graphic file, select the Graphics Tool and double-click on

Above: You can choose the image you want to use by bringing up the Open File dialog box.

the score. This brings up an Open File dialog, where you can navigate through your computer's file system and select the image file you want. The image will then appear where you clicked on the page.

Adjusting Your Graphic

Once the image is on the page, you can drag it to any position that you want. Alternatively, double-click to bring up the Graphics Attributes dialog, where you can set the position and size of the image on the page, and also the page range on which it will appear.

Linking or Embedding?

The Graphic Attributes dialog also lets you choose whether the Finale document will 'embed' the image within its file, or 'link' to the original graphic on your disk. Embedded images create larger Finale files, but they are more portable. Check or uncheck the 'Link To File' option.

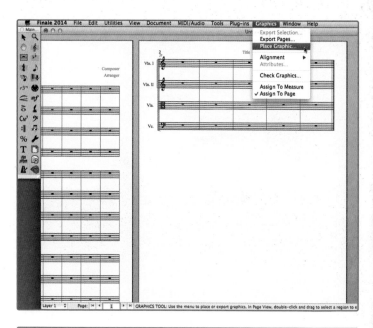

Above right: Choose this command from the Graphics menu to place your chosen graphic into your score.

Right: The Graphics Attributes contextual menu allows you to be specific about where and how your image will appear.

EDITING YOUR SCORE

EDITING YOUR SCORE

You've entered notes, articulations, dynamics, slurs and lyrics, chords and repeats. But there's still much more to be done. Finale has some powerful editing techniques that can really save you time.

Hot Tip

Double-clicking on various parts of the score will automatically change to the relevant tool.

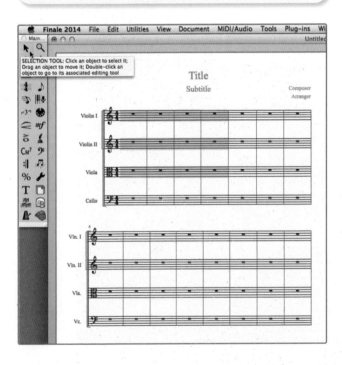

THE SELECTION TOOL

The main tool for editing in Finale is the Selection Tool. With this, you can highlight measures in your score and then manipulate them in various ways. You can cut, copy and paste. You can clear the contents. You can drag the contents of the selected region to other measures. You can perform a range of other functions on selected parts of the score.

Selecting Measures

You can select measures (bars) in a number of ways. You can 'drag a rectangle' across an area and all the measures inside will be selected. In the same way, you can select fractions of a measure to the nearest beat or note.

Left: To highlight measures with the Selection Tool, click outside and above the staff and drag diagonally across the measure or measures of your choice.

You can also click on a measure and Shift-click another measure, and all the measures in between will be selected.

Measure Stacks

If you select more than one staff, each staff is individually highlighted. If you select all the staves in one or more measures, then the highlighted area is continuous. This is known as a measure stack. There are differences in some behaviours between stacks and selections.

Hot Tip
Double-click to select a stack.

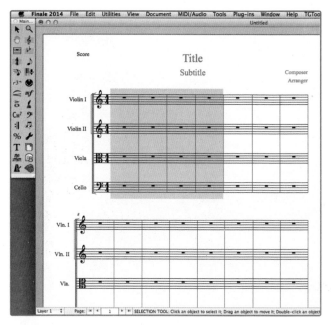

Above: A Measure Stack that has been selected.

Below: The Clear Selected Items dialog box lets you specify which elements of your score you want to remove.

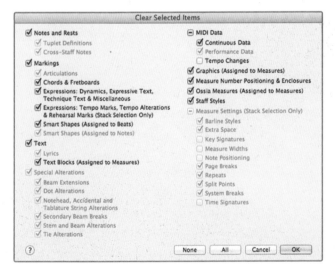

Cut, Copy and Paste

Like other apps, once you've selected something, you can cut, copy or paste it. If you select a measure stack, then cutting will delete the measures. If you select measures in some of the staves, then cutting will clear the measures. You can also drag the current selection to another location to copy its contents.

Hot Tip

You can paste the current selection to another location with Alt-click.

Clear Selected Items

As well as clearing the contents of a selected region, Finale lets you clear only particular types of notation. Click on 'Clear Selected Items...' from the Edit menu, and you'll get a dialog listing all the different types of symbol.

Paste Multiple

Finale has a feature that allows you to paste a selection repeatedly. This can be 'horizontally', repeating the

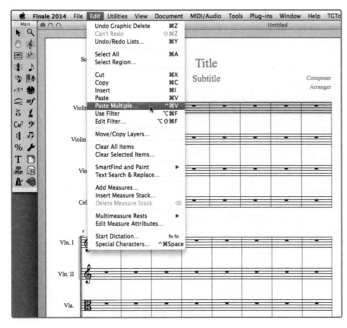

Above: Paste Multiple...

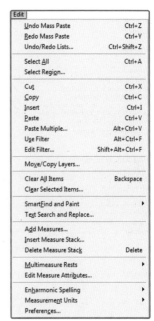

Above: Edit menu in Windows.

selection along the staff, or 'vertically', repeating the selection into other staves. 'Paste Multiple...' is in the Edit menu, and in the contextual right-click menu.

Insert

Pasting a selection into your score will overwrite the existing measures with the music from your selection. An alternative to pasting is to insert the contents of the clipboard. This will create new measures at the current selection point, moving the existing music to the right.

Filtering a Selection

With the filter, you can paste some, but not all, of the notation from a region. Select the Edit menu > Edit Filter, and choose the items you want to copy. 'Use Filter' in the Edit menu will now be checked. Now, when you paste or drag a selection, only the chosen items are copied.

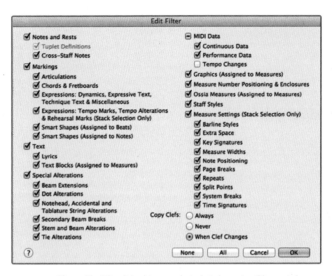

Above: The Filter dialog lets you select what elements will be copied.

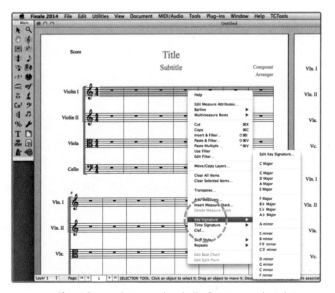

Above: Contextual menus, such as the Key Signature one shown here, give you a range of options you can use to edit elements of your score.

You can use this to copy expressions, articulations and even lyrics to another staff, or just copy the notes without the other details. Uncheck 'Use Filter' when you want to paste everything again.

Adding Measures

Finale has two options in the Edit menu: 'Add Measures', which adds measures to the end of the score, and 'Insert Measure Stack', which adds them to the left of the current selection. If you have a measure stack selected, then you can delete that stack from the score.

Click to the left of a staff to select all measures in the document.

Contextual Menu

Using the Selection Tool, you can right-click on a measure to reveal a range of options. You can change the clef, key or time signature for the selected region.

You can transpose the music, cut, copy or paste. The contextual menu is a very quick way of editing your score. Other tools will show different options in their contextual menus.

CHANGING ELEMENTS OF YOUR SCORE

Under the Utilities menu, there are several functions that you can use on a selected region of your score. The most useful ones are in the Change sub-menu. Here, you can perform global changes to notes, articulations, expressions, chords, ties and tuplets. The Utilities menu also has options for adjusting the stem direction of your notes, changing the instrument name and audio sample on a staff, and transposing your music. Most of these are as simple as selecting a region, clicking on the menu and selecting options in a dialog.

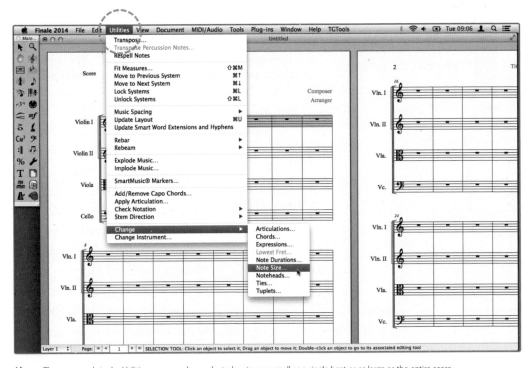

Above: The commands in the Utilities menu work on selected regions as small as a single beat or as large as the entire score.

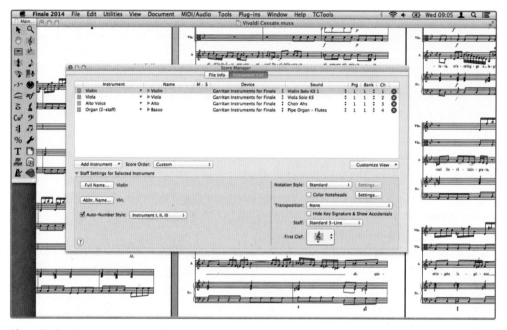

Above: The Score Manager lets you control the major characteristics of your score.

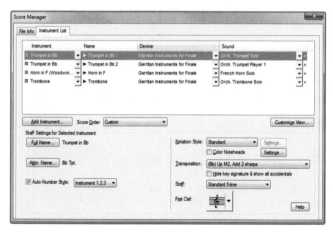

Above: The Windows version of the Score Manager.

SCORE MANAGER

The Score Manager lets you control various aspects of the score. It can be accessed through the Window menu. Using the Score Manager, you can change a variety of characteristics of each staff, such as its name, the sound sample used, the clef, transposition and notation style. You can also add staves, change the order of the staves, or delete staves.

If you have more than one of the same type of instrument, then Finale can automatically number the instruments (e.g. Violin I, Violin II ...), or you can turn off the numbering and give the instruments your own names. Full names are shown at the start of the piece, and abbreviated names used on every other system.

File Info

When creating a document using the Setup Wizard, there is a dialog for entering text fields, like the name of the composer, the title of the piece, the lyricist, copyright details and other information. If you need to change or add to this information later on, you can use the File Info dialog of the

Hot Tip

You can also edit a text field directly within a text box after you've inserted it.

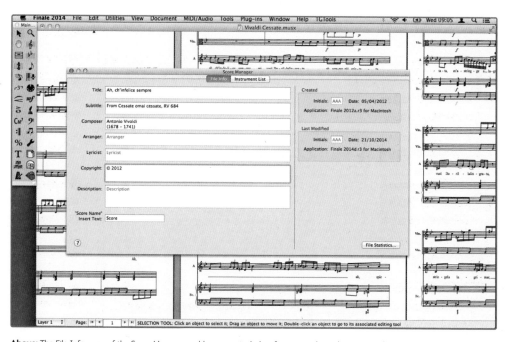

Above: The File Info pane of the Score Manager enables you to include information about the score, such as title and composer.

Score Manager. All the same fields are shown here as in the Setup Wizard, and these text fields can then be added to text boxes using the Insert sub-menu in the Text Tool's menu.

DOCUMENT OPTIONS

Finale has a vast array of settings in the Document Options dialog, where you can specify distances between objects, sizes, positions, fonts and other parameters of your document. There are settings for the spacing between accidentals, the size and shape of augmentation dots, and the thickness of barlines. You can create your own clefs or modify the existing ones. You can specify all the fonts that you want to use for different types of notation element. The interaction between music symbols can also be controlled.

It is here that you can truly control the fine detail required for professional-level music engraving, and also create special effects.

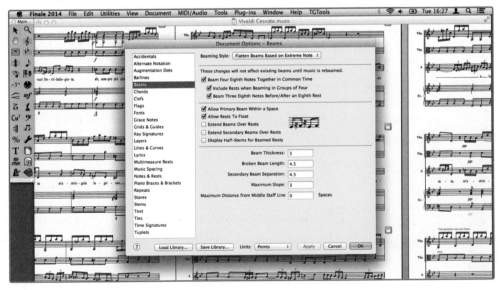

Above: The Document Options dialog box allows you make alterations to the global settings in your score, such as customizing beams, as shown here.

LAYING OUT YOUR SCORE

There's more to a score than just having all the notation symbols. The measures need to be laid out across a page, and the systems on each page need to be positioned for optimal use of the space.

OVERVIEW

Finale uses three of its tools for laying out your music on the page: the Selection Tool, the Staff Tool and the Page Layout Tool. These correspond to three separate tasks in layout: setting the number of measures on the system; spacing and hiding staves in each system; and spacing systems on each page. It's best to enter the notes first, and then lay the pages out.

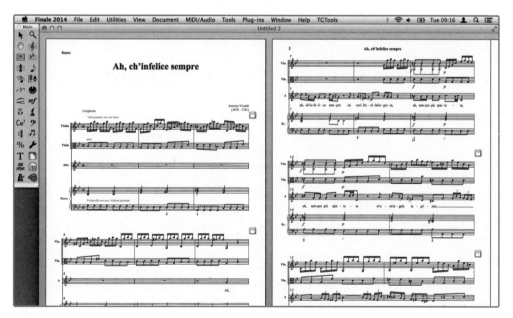

Above: A completed score in Finale, with expressions in green and layer 2 notes in red.

PAGE FORMAT

Finale bases every new page on the information in Document > Page Format > Score. This is where you set the page size, the page scaling, the staff size and the staff scaling. There are also settings for page margins and system margins, with different options for alternating pages and the first system. Changing these settings won't immediately do anything; you have to apply the changes to pages. This allows more than one format in a document. The changes are applied with the Page Layout Tool's 'Redefine Pages' menu item.

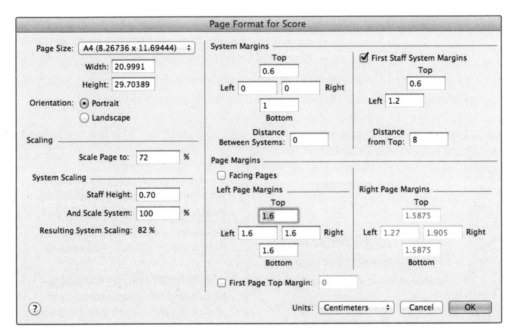

Above: Alter the page size, margins and the scale of the music, using the settings using the settings in the Page Format dialog box.

Locking the Systems

Normally, Finale automatically flows your measures on to each system of the score. However, it can reflow these measures as you work on the score, and you may want to make your own adjustments. The first step is to lock the measures to the systems, which will stop Finale moving them again. You can lock a system by selecting some measures in it with the Selection Tool and clicking on 'Lock Systems' in the Utilities menu. You can also unlock systems in the same menu. You'll see a padlock to the right of the system.

Above: Lock measures within a system to stop measures from reflowing across system breaks.

Fitting Measures to Systems

Instead of letting Finale decide how to divide the measures into systems, you might want to set a certain number of measures per system across the whole document. This is done with the 'Fit Music' command in the Utilities menu, which locks a set number of measures to each system in the selection. Select the region using the Selection Tool and click on 'Fit Measures' to set the number of measures per system. You can then specify how many measures you need. You can also fit the entire selection to one system, or remove system locks.

Hot Tip

To select the whole document, use Command + A (Mac) or Ctrl + A (PC).

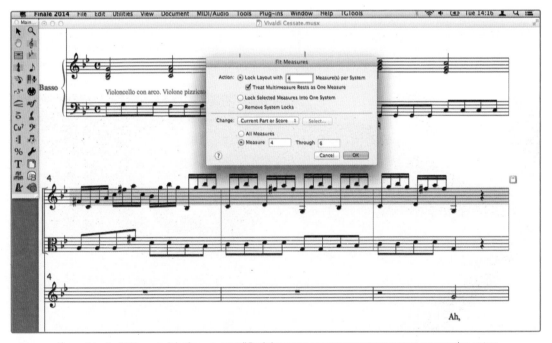

Above: Using the Fit Measures dialog box, you can tell Finale how many measures you want per system, among other options.

Manual Adjustment

Regardless of whether you let Finale lay the music out, or if you're using your own scheme, you might still want to make a few manual adjustments to the layout. One system might be too crowded with notes, and another might be stretched out too widely. Finale lets you move one or more measures from one system back on to the previous system, or forward on to the next. Select the measure(s) you want to move and press the up or down arrow. Moving measures in this way locks both systems. This is a very powerful but often overlooked feature of Finale that makes adjustments to systems easy.

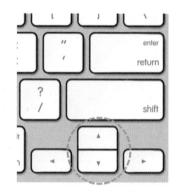

Above: You can edit your score manually, e.g. by moving measures out of a crowded system using the up or down arrows.

Above: When you drag a staff anchor, its distance from the staff above will appear.

SPACING STAVES

After setting out the measures per system, the next step is to space the staves with the Staff Tool. There are three different ways to adjust the spacing of staves: dragging, nudging or setting a value.

Dragging

Each staff has an anchor point on its top line at the left-hand end. You can drag this with your mouse pointer to space the staff. The distance to the staff above will be shown above the anchor point. Any staves below will hold their relative positions (so they will move too).

Nudging

With a staff's anchor point selected, use the up and down arrows to nudge the staff. If you want to adjust more than one system at once, then copy a measure region from one system to another. Select all the systems for that staff by clicking to the left of the staff.

Hot Tip

Hold down Alt (Mac) or Ctrl (PC) when you drag to hold the lower staves' positions.

Setting a Value

Dragging and nudging will work with only one staff. If you want to adjust more than one staff in one go, then you need to select a region (one or more staves, one or more systems), and then choose 'Respace Staves' from the Staff menu.

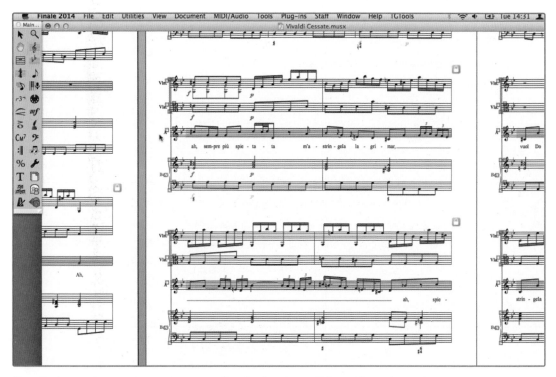

Above: To alter more than one system at a time, you must first select the region on which you wish to work.

LAYING OUT SYSTEMS

When you choose the Page Layout Tool, each system will have dotted lines showing the system margins. System margins are the area outside the staves that are reserved for that system. Normally, margins of adjacent systems will not collide with each other, so by setting the margins, you can define how much room each system has.

Adjusting System Margins

You can drag the anchor points on the margin corners to adjust the margins. Alternatively, you can use the dialog from the menu (Page Layout > Systems > Edit Margins) to set the margins of several staves to numerical values.

Dragging Systems

You can also drag an entire system, which will move the system on the page while maintaining its system margins. Just click within the staves and drag. This will affect other systems below, unless you hold Alt (Mac) or Ctrl (PC) while you drag.

Above: Use the Edit System Margins dialog box to set the margins of your systems numerically.

Distance Between Systems

As well as settings for system margins, the Edit Margins dialog contains settings for the distance between systems. You can select a range of systems and set the margins and distances all in one go.

Page Breaks

To make a system start on a new page, right-click in the system area and select 'Insert Page Break'. You can delete a page break from the same menu.

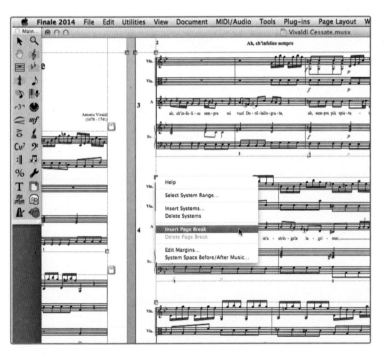

Above: Click on the Page Layout Tool and use the contextual menu to insert a page break.

Fitting Systems to Pages

The 'Space Systems Evenly' command in the Page Layout menu allows you to specify how many systems you want per page. It's easy to create a basic layout by applying this command to systems after setting suitable system margins.

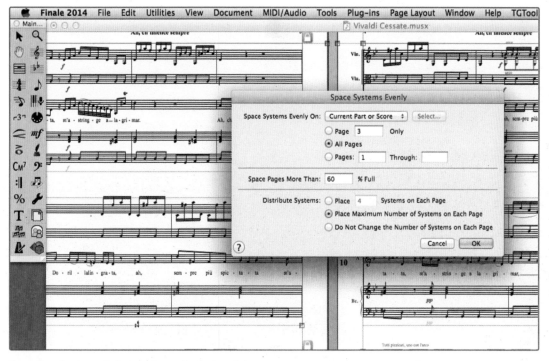

Above: Go to Page Layout Tool > Space Systems Evenly to specify how many systems you want per page, among other options.

Adding Blank Pages

The Page Layout menu has commands for creating and deleting blank pages in your score. They will stay free of music no matter what happens in your score. This can be useful for creating a title page and contents before the music, or editorial notes at the end. Choose 'Insert Blank Pages' from the Page Layout menu to add pages, or 'Delete Blank Pages' to remove them.

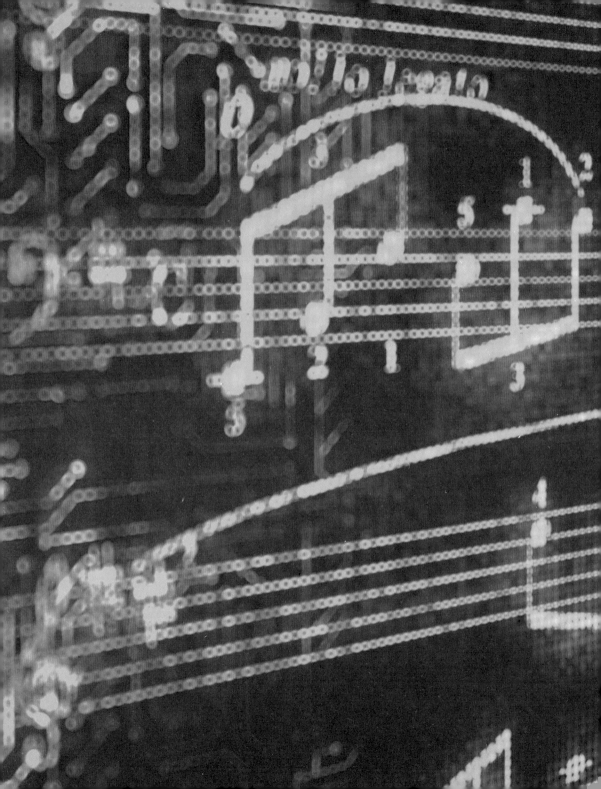

THE FINAL SCORE

THE FINAL SCORE

Once you've completed your score, what can you do with it? Printing it out might be the first answer, but Finale offers many more features for getting value from your finished documents.

OVERVIEW

As you might expect, Finale lets you print out your document, but it also includes some professional output options. You can also export a selected area, a page, or the whole document in a range of graphic file formats. Finale can play back your document using sophisticated audio samples, and export audio files of the playback. You can export to other formats, to use your music in other programs.

PRINTING

Finale prints your documents much like any other app. Just select 'Print' from the File menu, and all your printer's options will be available. However, there are a couple of extra features. Firstly, Finale will ask you which section of the document you want to print: you can select the score and each part individually or all of them together. Finale also has special options which appear in your print dialog. Some of these are the same as other options that you might have elsewhere in your Print menu. Others are more specialized.

The options are:

- **Left & right**: Left pages, right pages, or left and right pages.

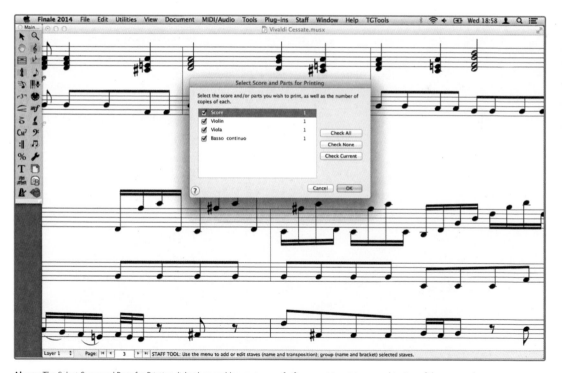

Above: The Select Score and Parts for Printing dialog box enables you to specify if you want to print any combination of the score and parts.

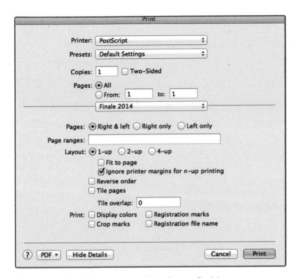

Above: The Print dialog as seen on a Mac, showing Finale's own print options.

Above: The Print dialog as seen in Windows, showing Finale's own print options.

○ **Specified pages:** A list of pages separated by a comma, or a range separated by a dash (e.g. 11-22).

○ **1-up, 2-up and 4-up:** Allows you to print more than one page per sheet.

○ **Ignore printer margins:** Makes multiple pages on a sheet as big as possible.

○ **Reverse order:** Start printing from last to first.

○ **Tile pages:** One page on many sheets; there's also an overlap setting.

○ **Display colors:** Includes Finale's onscreen colours.

○ **Crop marks:** Pages can be printed on oversized sheets, with marks to show where the page edges are.

○ **Registration marks and filename:** These are used in preparing files for printing presses.

EXPORTING

Finale can export data from your documents for use in other applications.
It can export images of your music, or it can export the actual musical data.

EXPORTING GRAPHICS

Finale has its own methods for exporting pages or selected areas of pages in PDF, EPS, JPEG, TIFF, SVG or PNG format. It's easy to do this.

1. With the Graphics Tool selected, use the 'Export Pages' command to export one or more pages. (Each page will be saved as a separate file, except for PDFs.)

2. Double-click and drag to select an area on the page that you want to export.

Above: To export part of a score as a graphic, first select the area, then go to Graphics Tool > Export Selection.

Above: Choose which format you'd like your graphic to be from the Graphics Export dialog box.

3. Finally, choose 'Export Selection' from the Graphics menu and choose the type of format you'd like your graphic to be in.

Above: The Graphics Export dialog box as seen on a Windows PC.

EXPORTING MUSIC

Finale can export the data in your document as a MIDI file, as MusicXML and even as an ePub file for viewing on an ebook reader. MIDI files can then be imported into Digital Audio Workstations (DAWs), like Cubase, ProTools or Logic. MusicXML is an interchange format between notation software. There is increasing support for this format, which can already be used to exchange files with Sibelius, MuseScore and many other programs. Exporting music as an ebook makes

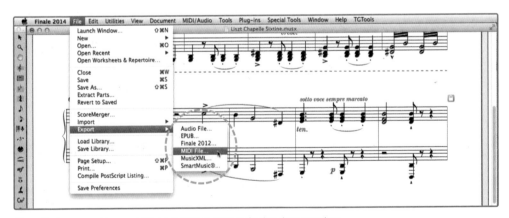

Above: Finale can export to several different formats, as shown in the drop-down menu here.

the music accessible to a wide audience. (There is also an iPad app, Finale SongBook, for viewing Finale files directly.) The File > Export menu has the options for these formats.

Libraries

You may want to reuse some of your settings, chords, expressions and articulations within another document. You can do this by saving a library from one document and loading it into another. 'Load Library' and 'Save Library' commands are in the File menu.

Clip Files

You can save selected regions of a document to your hard drive as 'clip files'. These can be as little as a single beat in one measure, or as much as an entire document. You can cut, copy, paste or insert clip files using the same edit commands for cut, copy, paste and insert, while holding down Ctrl (Windows) or Alt (Mac).

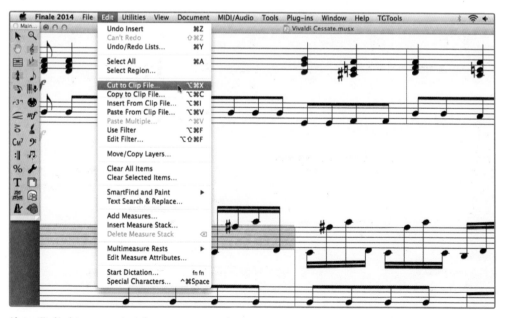

Above: Clip files let you save extracts from your score to use in other projects.

PLAYBACK

Finale has advanced features for playing back your music. It can use high-quality audio samples and sophisticated techniques for incorporating different performance effects.

OVERVIEW

Just press the play button on the Playback Controls to hear your music. Finale will scroll through the music as it plays, showing you the current 'playhead' position with a green line. The program will incorporate the dynamics, articulations and expressions that you've used into the 'performance', and

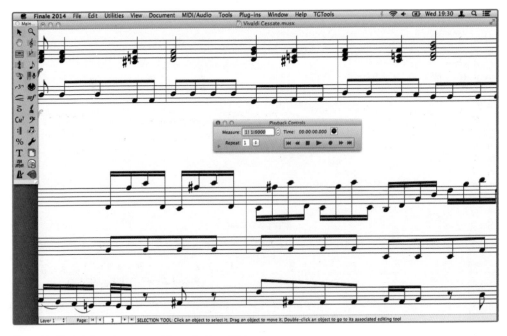

Above: The Playback Controls are accessed from a floating palette.

will also obey any repeat instructions in your score. There is also a feature called Human Playback, which interprets the music according to a series of rules, making the playback less robotic.

SOUND LIBRARIES

Finale can use several different sound libraries, and will find a sample to match each instrument from what is available. So if a friend has another sound library, you can share the document and it will use the correct sample on each computer without you needing to change the document. In any document created in the Setup Wizard, each staff will be assigned audio samples, based on the name of the instrument. You can see the assigned samples in the Score Manager (from the Window menu). If you have more than one sound library, you can set your preferred order in MIDI/Audio > Sound Map Priority.

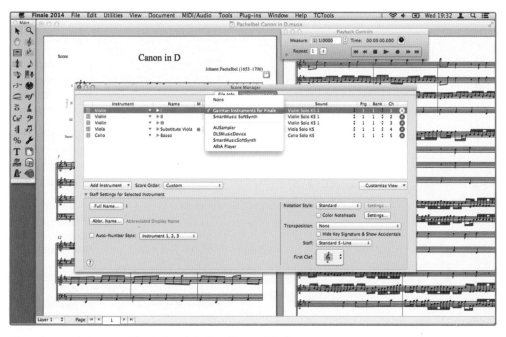

Above: You can select your sound libraries through the Score Manager dialog box.

Reassigning Playback Sounds

If you want to change the sample library used in your score,
then set the Sound Map Priority in the MIDI/Audio menu to the
order in which you want your libraries to be selected, then
select 'Reassign Playback Sounds'. Finale will look at each
instrument in the score and assign the default sound
for that instrument. Finale comes with two sample
libraries: SmartMusic SoftSynth, a basic General
MIDI sample library; and Garritan Instruments for
Finale, a much more professional library, with a wide
range of instruments. You can also change the sound library
and sound used individually in the Score Manager.

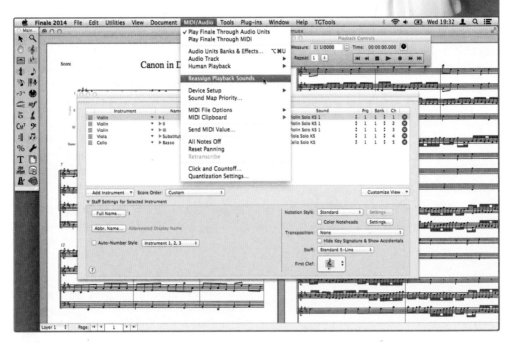

Above: Choose this option to change the entire sample library that your score uses.

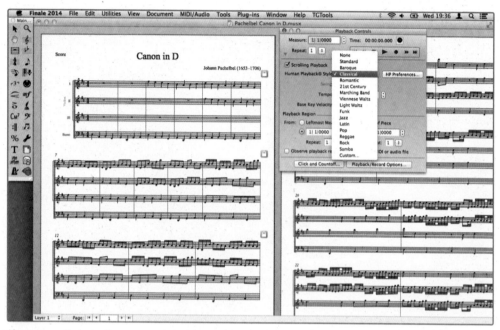

Above: Human Playback settings generate playback that simulates a live, less robotic, 'human' performance.

HUMAN PLAYBACK

Finale uses the information in your score to affect the playback. Dynamics, slurs and articulations, such as staccato marks and fermatas, will all be observed. Text expressions, such as *rit*, *cresc*, *pizzicato*, will be adhered to in playback. Numeric metronome indications in Tempo Marks will be used in the score. Finale will also slow down before final barlines. A range of different styles, from Baroque to Swing, can be selected, which make the playback less robotic and more 'human'. Clicking on the little arrow in the bottom-left corner of the Playback Controls window reveals a range of playback options. More advanced settings that affect Human Playback can be found in the application's preferences.

ADVANCED FINALE

ADVANCED FINALE

Finale is a very complex program, and we have barely scratched the surface of its capabilities. Let's look in more depth at some of its more advanced features.

OVERVIEW

There are many more features that make Finale one of the leading music notation software apps, which

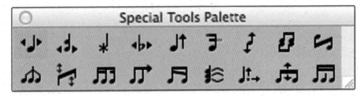

Above: Advanced notational effects can be achieved with the Special Tools Palette.

can be used to produce highly professional results. Finale has another group of tools in their own tool palette, the Special Tools, for making fine manual adjustments to the notation. There is also a menu for plug-ins – additional components that provide more features. The app has its own scripting language for automating repetitive tasks, and there is a plethora of document options to customize the look of the music on the page.

SPECIAL TOOLS

The Special Tools are a range of 18 tools for making fine adjustments to your notation. Select the tool you need to use and then click on a measure. You will see anchor points on the object that the tool controls, and you can make the adjustments by hand. With these tools, you can change individual elements of the score, without making global changes, in Document Options.

Hot Tip

Make sure you're in the correct layer when using Special Tools.

Special Tools Palette   Special Tools Palette Menu

Special
Tool
Icon

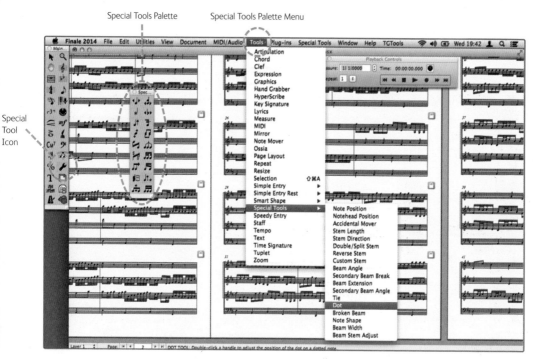

Above: Use the Special Tools Palette and menu to make fine adjustments to your score.

Double-clicking on anchor points in some tools brings up a menu, where attributes can be changed and positions specified by set distances. Other tools work purely by manual adjustment.

Tools for Adjusting Notes

There are six tools for altering the position, shape and size of notation symbols:

 Note Position Tool: Adjusts the horizontal position of the entire note or chord.

 Notehead Position Tool: Moves an individual notehead only, leaving the stem and other noteheads.

 Note Shape Tool: Changes the notehead to another music symbol.

Accidental Tool: Defines the position, size, font and symbol for an accidental.

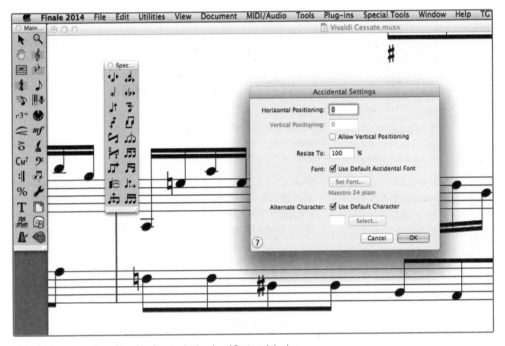

Above: Adjust the position of accidentals using the Accidental Settings dialog box.

 Tie Tool: This gives three anchor points on each tie, allowing you to adjust the position and curve of the tie.

 Dot Tool: Adjusts the horizontal and vertical position of an augmentation dot.

Tools for Adjusting Stems

There are six tools for altering the characteristics of note stems:

 Stem Length Tool: Adjusts the length and position of a single stem.

 Stem Direction Tool: Defines whether a stem goes above or below the notehead.

 Double/Split Stem Tool: Creates stems on both sides of the note. Also breaks stems within chords. This allows the appearance of two voices without using layers.

 Reverse Stem Tool: Moves the stem to the other side of the note.

 Custom Stem Tool: Replaces the stem with a graphical shape.

 Beam Stem Adjust Tool: Adjusts the position of stems within beam groups.

Below: Go to Special Tools > Double/Split Stem Tool to create stems on both sides of the notes.

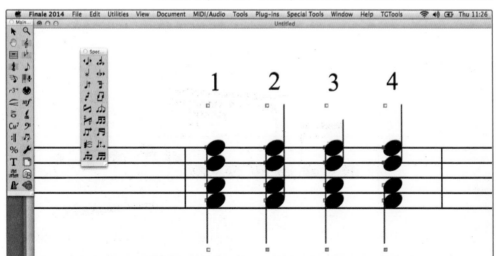

Tools for Adjusting Beams

There are six tools for adjusting the position, size and shape of beamed groups (notes that are joined together):

 Broken Beam Tool: Flips a broken secondary beam to the other side of a stem.

 Beam Angle Tool: Adjusts the angle of a primary beam.

 Secondary Beam Break Tool: Breaks secondary beams.

 Beam Extension Tool: Extends beams horizontally beyond the last note of the group.

 Secondary Beam Angle Tool: Adjusts the angle of a secondary beam.

 Beam Width Tool: Alters the thickness of all beams in a group.

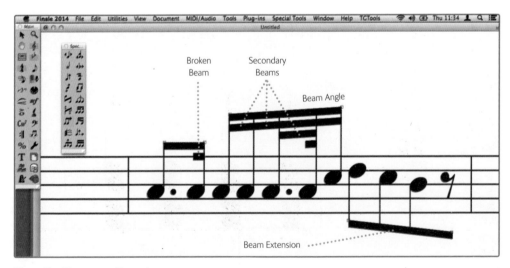

Above: The different parts of beamed notes.

PLUG-INS

Finale comes with a large collection of plug-ins. These are external additions to the program that give extra features and functions. The plug-ins can all be found in their own menu, arranged into different categories. Third-party plug-ins, which you can download, can provide significant enhancements to your productivity. Some of the most useful plug-ins are:

- **Patterson Beams**: Adjusts beam angles to achieve a more professional result.

- **Cautionary Accidentals**: Adds 'warning' accidentals to the score.

- **Auto Slur Melismas**: Places slurs over lyric melismas.

- **Space Systems**: Gives enhanced controls for spacing systems.

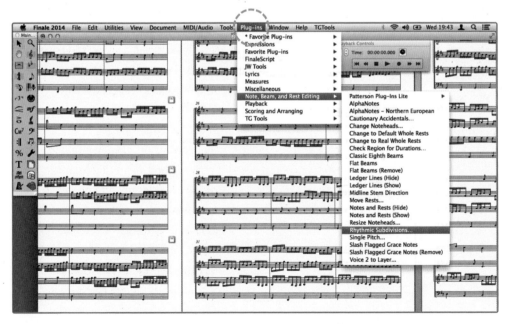

Above: Plug-ins are very useful, and operate on the entire document or on a specified region.

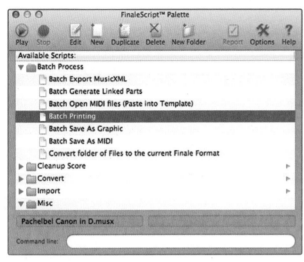

Above: Use the script shown here – Batch Printing – to print many documents at the same time.

Above: You can edit existing scripts, or even create new ones: go to Plug-ins > FinaleScript > FinaleScript Palette.

○ **Vertical Collision Remover**: Re-spaces staves in a system according to contents.

○ **Score System Divider**: Adds marks to highlight the division between systems on a page.

FINALESCRIPT

Finale comes with its own scripting language, FinaleScript, which is located in the Plug-ins menu. It can be used to automate repetitive sequences into one click of a button. Several scripts are already included, and you can batch-process Finale documents, moving the processed files to another folder.

Script Options

There are scripts already included for batch printing, exporting to other formats, and for reformatting your documents to another page size. You can create your own scripts for any process that you perform regularly in Finale. Scripts are just a sequence of commands: there's no heavy logic and you don't need programming skills to use them.

MEASURE NUMBERING

You can configure your document to display measure numbers in a variety of ways: on each staff, on the top of the system, in a set position or at regular intervals.

Regions

This is all done from the 'Edit Measure Number Regions' command in the Document menu. Each region that you define (from one measure to another) can have its own settings. By default, Finale places measure numbers on the left-hand side of the system, on top of each instrumental group. Creating more than one region allows sections of your score to each have their own numbering scheme, or you can have two regions in the same measures, to display two different number styles.

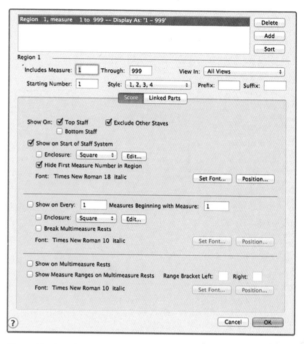

Above: Use the Measure Number dialog box to define measure numbering for your score and parts.

OTHER TOOLS

There are several other tools on the main palette that we've not explored, such as the Ossia, Mirror, Note Mover, MIDI, Tempo and Tuplet tools. It is possible to use Finale fully without using these tools. The Note Mover Tool is the most useful for cross-staff notes in piano parts.

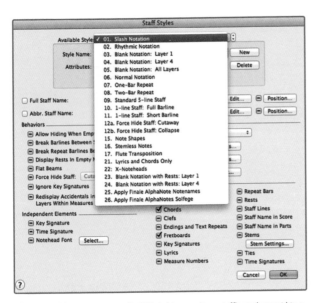

Above: Assigning a Staff Style lets you alter a staff's attributes within a region of the score.

STAFF STYLES

Another feature of the Staff Tool is Staff Styles, where attributes of the staff can be applied to a selected region. Using Staff Styles, you can hide individual measures within a system, or change the staff's name temporarily. Styles can be 'Defined', 'Applied' or 'Cleared' (removed) using the Staff Tool's menu. Very advanced effects can be created with Staff Styles.

METATOOLS

Finale has many keyboard shortcuts, covering most of its options and choices. A Metatool is simply the keyboard equivalent of a certain expression marking; you simply press a letter or number key on your keyboard instead of going through a complicated process involving dialog boxes and mouse clicks.

Expression & Articulations

There are Metatools for selecting many of the default articulations and expressions, for choosing a new time or key signature, for entering notes in Simple Entry and for adding chords. You can define your own Metatool for articulations:

1. Hold Shift down and press the key you want to use.

2. Select the articulation in the Selection dialog.

3. The same process works for expressions.

There's a complete list of default shortcuts and Metatools in Finale's own Help files.

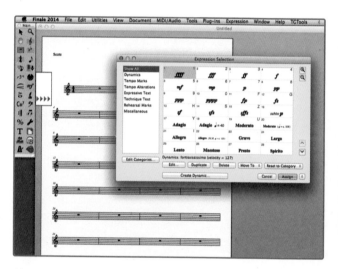

Above: The metatool assigned to each expression is shown in the right-hand corner of each item in the Expressions Selection dialog.

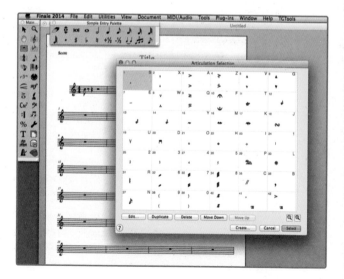

Above: The metatool assigned to each articulation is shown in the right-hand corner of each item in the Articulation Selection dialog.

Hot Tip

Press hyphen and click to use the same expression, articulation or chord again.

CUSTOMIZATION

Finale comes with four different music notation fonts: Jazz and Broadway, which give a handwritten look; and Maestro and Engraver, which give an 'engraved' look. However, Finale can use many other third-party music symbol fonts, including those used by other notation apps.

Change the Default Font

There's an option in the Document menu to change the music font, if you'd rather use another one:

1. Go to Document > Set Default Music Font.

2. Choose the new font and style, and click OK twice.

3. You will also need a 'FAN' – a Font ANnotation file – that tells Finale about the font. Finale will create one if it is missing.

By changing the music font, and the text fonts used for other elements of the score, as well as other settings in Document Options, you can create a unique house style for your music.

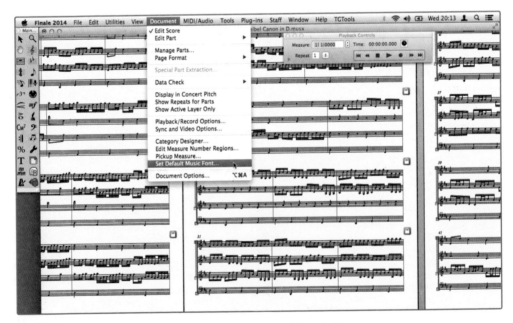

Above: Finale can use a range of different music fonts, to giove your music a different look.

HELP FILES

This book is designed to cover the basics of Finale and help you to understand its key features and methods. However, the software comes with comprehensive documentation. There are videos that introduce many of the key concepts. There are tutorial documents that take you step-by-step through different tasks, and there are webpages that list every function and tell you what every setting in every dialog does.

Online Help

The Help files also have lists of all the shortcuts and Metatools. MakeMusic's Finale installs the documentation on to your computer, but while you have an internet connection, it will use the updated files on MakeMusic's own website.

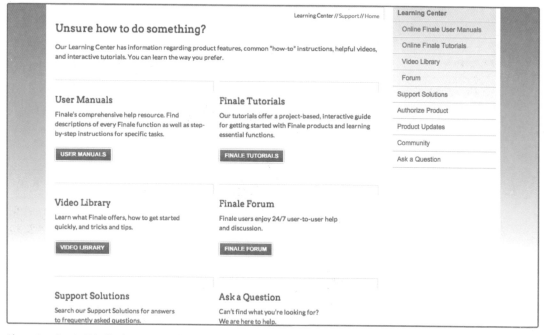

Above: As well as the Help files that come with the app, MakeMusic's website contains a wealth of information on using Finale.

USEFUL WEBSITES AND FURTHER READING

WEBSITES

finaletips.nu
A great website, packed with free plug-ins, fonts, tips and tricks, and challenges to test your Finale skills.

www.finaleforum.com
Discussion forum for Finale users.

forum.makemusic.com
User forum, maintained by MakeMusic, the makers of Finale.

FURTHER READING

Finale 2014: A Trailblazer Guide, by Mark Johnson. Penelope Press, 978-0981473178.

Behind Bars, by Elaine Gould. Faber Music, 9780571514564.

Music Engraving Today: The Art and Practice of Digital Notesetting, by Steven Powell, 9780965891011.

INDEX